ESSAYS ON THE MEXICAN REVOLUTION

The Walter Prescott Webb Memorial Lectures: XIII

BY

WILLIAM H. BEEZLEY

FRIEDRICH KATZ

DOUGLAS W. RICHMOND

DAVID C. BAILEY

LYLE C. BROWN

Sponsored by The University of Texas at Arlington

Essays on the Mexican Revolution

Revisionist Views of the Leaders

Introduction by Michael C. Meyer

Edited by

George Wolfskill

and Douglas W. Richmond

UNIVERSITY OF TEXAS PRESS

AUSTIN AND LONDON

Library of Congress Cataloging in Publication Data

Main entry under title:
Essays on the Mexican Revolution.

(The Walter Prescott Webb memorial lectures; 13)
Lectures given on Mar. 16, 1978, at the University of Texas at Arlington.
1. Mexico—History—1910–1946—Addresses, essays, lectures. I. Beezley, William H. II. Wolfskill, George, 1921– III. Richmond, Douglas W., 1946– IV. Series.
F1234.E795 972.08 79-12588
ISBN 0-292-72026-2

Printed in the United States of America

TO ROBERT W. AMSLER

Contents

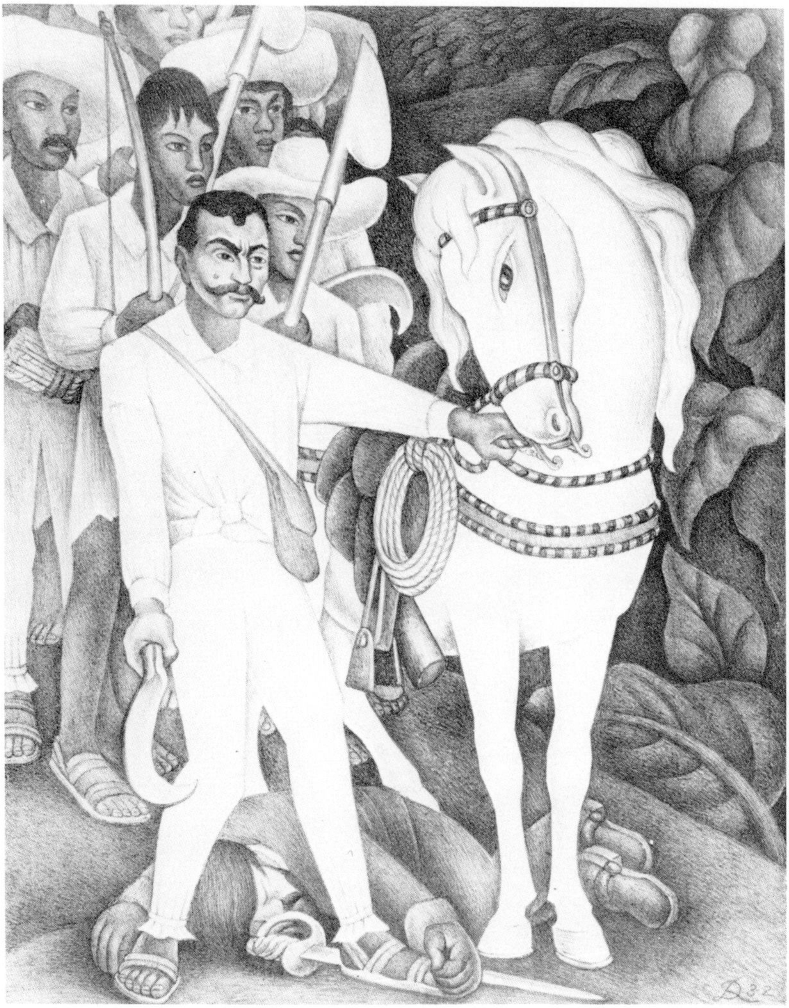

Zapata by Diego Rivera

Zapatistas by José Clemente Orozco

Equilibrio by Jesús Escobedo

Stevedores by Pablo O'Higgins

The Orator by Pablo O'Higgins

All illustrations in this section courtesy of Weyhe Gallery, New York

Preface

GEORGE WOLFSKILL AND DOUGLAS W. RICHMOND

On March 16, 1978, the University of Texas at Arlington was host for the thirteenth annual Walter Prescott Webb Memorial Lectures. Those guests who attended heard the lecturers discuss the evolution of policies and attitudes that still linger within the leadership of today's Mexico. They also enjoyed an impressive art exhibit of Mexican lithographs, some of which are reproduced in this volume, and felt the emotions of the Mexican Revolution as expressed by that country's leading artists.

Walter Prescott Webb would have enjoyed this series of essays on Mexico's revolutionary leaders because some of Webb's own work analyzed Mexico within the context of his ideas on frontiers and societies in change. Webb was puzzled by the momentous events that shook Mexico from 1910 to 1940. Not only interminable revolution and turmoil but also border assaults, oil seizures, threats of war, race riots, widespread emigration, and determined efforts to end United States economic privileges in Mexico were some of the more prominent issues that concerned Webb and Texas during those troubled years.

Despite the impressive amount of research and writing on the Mexican Revolution in recent years, much controversy continues and crucial questions still remain unresolved. The nature and quality of Mexican revolutionary leadership is one of those questions. These four lectures, which the authors have revised in varying degrees in order to strengthen the published version, and a prize-winning essay address themselves to that question. The results are new and sometimes startling reinterpretations of Francisco Madero, Venustiano Carranza, Alvaro Obregón, Pancho Villa, and Lázaro Cárdenas. Readers of this volume will discover not only a series of stimulating essays, but also challenging new insights that are, in most instances, the beginning of major studies.

In describing Madero's generally inept attempt to form a popular following in the countryside, Professor William Beezley from North Carolina State University at Raleigh makes Madero out to be something far less than his traditional image as the democratic martyr of the Revolution. Villa, who is generally considered a destructive brute, receives a sympathetic analysis from Professor Friedrich Katz of the University of Chicago who points out the strengths of Villa's reforms in Chihuahua. Professor Douglas Richmond of the host institution for these lectures, the University of Texas at Arlington, attacks the notion that Carranza was a tired conservative. He maintains that Carranza was a fierce nationalist who enjoyed mass support because of his early socioeconomic reforms. Professor David Bailey of Michigan State University portrays Obregón, not as the steady reformer that so many historians claim he was, but simply as a leader who cared less for principles than for order and accommodation. Finally, Professor Lyle Brown of Baylor University, winner of the Webb-Smith essay competition, demonstrates that Cárdenas wanted *campesino* support so as to minimize his dependence on politicians, bureaucrats, organized labor, and the military.

The essays in this volume, then, are sometimes amusing, sometimes moving, occasionally contradictory, and often aggravating; but they all have one thing in common: They challenge current thinking and, in the process, add something new and important to twentieth-century Mexican history.

This volume is dedicated to Robert W. Amsler, professor of history at the University of Texas at Arlington, who died June 19, 1977. Born in McGregor, Texas, Professor Amsler attended the University of Texas at Austin where he studied under Walter Webb and received the doctorate in 1950. Professor Amsler came to Arlington in 1957. He supported enthusiastically the Webb Lectures and was a contributor to the seventh volume. Professor Amsler was a good teacher, a loyal friend and colleague, an altogether decent man. There are those of us who continue to miss him.

George Wolfskill
Douglas W. Richmond

Introduction

MICHAEL C. MEYER

After years of careful study, the Mexican Revolution remains interesting. The inherent fascination of the Revolution continues as students, scholars, amateur historians, and the larger United States public are attracted in increasing numbers.

The reasons are myriad. Erupting in 1910, seven years before the Russian Revolution, the Mexican upheaval was, after all, the first profound social movement of the twentieth century. Some of the most momentous battles were fought on the very border of the United States. The list of unforgettable historical characters is impressive, extending well beyond the two most memorable—Pancho Villa and Emiliano Zapata.

At the outbreak of the Revolution, Mexicans had just gone through the thirty-four–year dictatorship of Porfirio Diaz. This soldier-politician had succeeded in bringing law and order to a country hitherto remarkable primarily for its political chaos, had attracted foreign capital where none would previously invest, had modernized a country that had been economically retrogressive, and had fostered the growth of a new middle class in urban areas heretofore typified by the stereotyped polarity between rich and poor. The philosophical underpinning was Mexican-style positivism, championed by an elite group of intellectuals known as Científicos. The changes that occurred in Mexico from 1876 to 1910 were genuinely extraordinary.

The costs of these profound changes, however, were substantial and it was against these costs that Mexicans reacted in 1910. Political corruption was rampant; the jails were filled with political prisoners; the newspapers were censored;

recalcitrant editors were imprisoned, fined, exiled, or even killed. Foreign capitalists had a free hand to do what they wanted; the profits from their investments all left the country, but the costs were borne equally by the masses who lived in rural Mexico. Through a variety of machinations, land was seized from the peasantry and their modest incomes declined just as prices rose. In essence, Díaz had developed his country at the expense of his countrymen. The material benefits of his age of modernization in no way filtered down to the people.

The fight against the Díaz dictatorship was won with amazing rapidity. In barely six months (November 1910 to May 1911) a ragtag rebel fighting force humbled Mexico's professionally trained and well-equipped federal army. The revolutionary contingents were not the stereotypical peasant army portrayed in the popular literature. There were peons to be sure; but in addition, servants, shopkeepers, mechanics, beggars, unemployed miners, federal army deserters, lawyers, United States and European soldiers of fortune, young and old, bandits and idealists, students and teachers, engineers and day laborers, the bored and the overworked, the aggrieved and the adventuresome, all constituted the rank and file.

Some were attracted by commitment to the cause and some by the promise of spoils. Some joined impulsively and others only with careful forethought. Some envisioned simply the overthrow of a despotic regime, others wanted a modest reorientation of society, and still others held out for a complete restructuring of the social order. Initially a source of strength, this tremendous diversity of interest and motivation would soon spell disaster.

The capture of Ciudad Juárez in May 1911 and the subsequent resignation of the dictator occasioned thunderous celebrations throughout the country; but the conviviality and jubilee soon gave way to acrimonious debate when the victorious rebels could not agree upon what it was they had won. When Porfirio Díaz sailed away to his European exile, the one bond that had cemented the rebel movement disappeared and the revolutionary coalition immediately began to fragment. As the victors began to fight among themselves for the spoils it became apparent that an old age had ended without a new one beginning.

The Mexico of 1910 to 1920 was not a place for the squeamish. With revolts and counterrevolts, with military coups, with rapid changes in the presidential chair, and with political assassinations and mass executions, the catharsis was slow in coming. By any standard the loss of life was staggering. Accurate statistics are not available, but no less than a million and a half (and perhaps two million) lost their lives in those ten terrible years. In a country with a population of approximately fifteen million in 1910 about one out of every eight Mexicans was killed, and few families did not directly feel the anguish. Even Mexico's high birthrate failed to offset the casualties of war. The census takers in 1920 counted almost a million fewer Mexicans than they had counted a decade before.

A cost so outrageous exacted burning resentment and tremendous fear in the civilian population. An approaching military unit, no matter what the affiliation, invariably meant trouble for the poor rural Mexican. The best that could be hoped for was a small band demanding a meal, but the extortions of war were generally more exorbitant. As is the case with most civil conflicts, this one did not lend itself easily to humanity or compassion. The sight of burning buildings and the nausea of mass burials brought home in tangible terms the most immediate meaning of the Revolution. In the northern part of the country tens of thousands of rural Mexicans fled across the border to the sanctuary of the United States. In central and southern Mexico there was virtually no place to run. Civilians kept their heads low and resigned themselves to the worst.

The decade of violence left little time for refashioning the contours of society, but even during the period of utmost chaos certain unstructured social change was occurring in Mexico. Internal migration took place, northerners and southerners came into more frequent contact with one another, distinct regional language patterns began to yield to a more homogeneous national tongue. Increased travel, even though it might have been occasioned by forced military conscription, provided a broader conception and deeper appreciation of Mexico. Greater physical mobility increased miscegenation and began to homogenize previously isolated zones. Thousands of Mexicans escaped obscurity and rose to positions of tremendous power. Even though many did not exercise their newly found influence with moderation, for them the decade of violence was an agent of social change.

Certainly by 1920, a new kind of revolutionary nationalism had begun to emerge—perhaps it started in 1917, with the promulgation of the new constitution or perhaps in 1918 or 1919 when the violence began to recede under President Venustiano Carranza. In any case, the dead heroes had become martyrs to a young generation of Mexicans who did not always realize that their favorite protagonists had been killed fighting one another. The heroes loomed larger in death than in life and their errors of judgment and human frailties could be overlooked. More important than the creation of the pantheon of heroes, the base of power in the country had shifted into new hands and Mexico was on the threshold of better times. The violence was not yet completely spent, but the struggles in the post-1920 period became less chaotic and more deliberative as national politicians found more constructive releases for their energy and fervor.

Between 1920 and 1940, the lives of average Mexicans changed more rapidly than they had in any previous twenty-year period. The population decline of the violent era stopped, and, with the relative political stability of the 1920s and 1930s, the population again began to rise. When Lázaro Cárdenas turned over the sash of office to his successor in 1940, the population of Mexico had reached twenty million, six million more than when Alvaro Obregón had assumed office twenty years earlier.

Mexico was still a rural country when Cárdenas's term ended, and it was in rural Mexico that the change in life-style was most dramatic. Seventy-five million acres of land had been distributed since 1910 (fifty million alone during the Cárdenas years). The percentage of people who wore neither shoes nor sandals declined as did the percentage of illiterates. By 1940, cultural anthropologists found it difficult to find any of those quaint Indians who spoke a native tongue to the complete exclusion of Spanish. The new *ejidatario* in rural Mexico, unlike his peon forefather, was no longer bound to the hacienda. He could travel as freely as his pocketbook allowed.

Thousands of Mexicans who had fled their villages during the early Revolution returned to find that some impressive changes were taking place. Blacktop highways began to replace bumpy dirt roads, and buses rolled over them with more or less regularity. Bicycles began to push burros off the highways. Tractors did not displace but at least challenged the ox-drawn plow. Gasoline engines, rather than mules or horses, turned the mills that ground the corn. Gasoline pumps drew the water from nearby streams. Electricity arrived even in some small towns.

The most important change, however, was the new rural school which, by the late 1930s, had become the focal point of village life. Economic and social activity centered on programs initiated by the rural teacher. Cultural life for the first time was dominated more by the school than the church. With the gradual extension of medical facilities into the village, life expectancy improved and the infant mortality rate dropped from 222 deaths per thousand in 1920 to 125 twenty years later. By no means did all of the requisites of the good life come to rural Mexico between 1920 and 1940, but by the latter date it was no longer accurate to suggest that rural Mexicans continued to live as they had since the days of the Spanish conquest.

Life in the cities changed as well. Organized labor emerged as a force to be reckoned with as its campaigns to improve salaries and working conditions encountered moderate success. Working-class interests could never again be completely overlooked. With the amenities of technology, city life became more pleasant. Perhaps of greatest significance by 1940, as the shock of the carnage receded into the past, Mexicans had begun to think of themselves differently. Pride in the progress of change replaced the national shame of the early twentieth century. Contributing most to the growing sense of nationalism was Lázaro Cárdenas's decision to nationalize the foreign-owned oil companies in March 1938. His nationalization decree immediately became a cause célèbre. By striking this sharp blow for Mexican economic independence, Cárdenas fired the patriotism of an entire generation of Mexicans.

Although Mexico was not an idyllic world in 1940, it would be folly to gainsay the changes that had occurred in the previous thirty years. They were sufficiently remarkable to legitimate that much overworked adjective *revolutionary*.

The processes of change, however, were wrought with difficulty. A revolution simply is not won by good intentions. Successes are often balanced with failures, and trade-offs in one area are the price for victory in another.

The five essays that make up this volume examine those complicated revolutionary processes and emphasize the successes and failures of the movement during the period 1910 to 1940. In a fresh and imaginative way William Beezley examines the Madero phase of the Revolution. Using as his point of departure Luis González's delightful anecdote of Elías Martínez, the would-be Birdman of San José de Gracia, Beezley probes the meaning of the Madero movement at the state and local level. If the villagers of San José de Gracia considered Martínez's attempted flight more significant than Madero's Revolution, it had to be because Madero had neither delivered an adequate message nor implemented a constructive program for rural Mexico. A Revolution launched in part against the excessive centralization of the Porfiriato fell easy victim to the undeniable attractions of state autonomy and the *municipio libre*. While a few state governors instituted reform programs above and beyond that envisioned in Madero's own Plan de San Luis Potosí, a coherent and integrated program of rural regeneration was remarkable only for its absence during the first elected government to emanate from the Revolution.

To celebrate the one-hundredth anniversary of Villa's birth, the Mexican government declared 1978 to be the "Year of General Francisco Villa." While Villa's role in the official ideology of the Revolution thus seemed assured, Pancho Villa, the historical figure, continues to evoke polemic and passion. Friedrich Katz, as part of a larger biographical enterprise, has here chosen one aspect of Villa's multifaceted career to dispel some myths. Villa's governorship in Chihuahua in 1913 and 1914 not only has considerable intrinsic interest to the student of the Mexican Revolution but, in addition, helps to refute part of the corpus of anti-Villa mythology.

What emerges in Katz's most careful analysis is a state administration characterized not by plunder and pillage but by a reasoned approach to difficult revolutionary challenges. Given a series of countervailing pressures, Villa was able to finance a military movement, attack the entrenched Mexican oligarchy, and maintain cordial relations with the United States. In the short run, the *villista* state government must be judged a success; but Professor Katz tantalizingly posits in his conclusion that these same immediate victories may have contained the seeds of Villa's ultimate demise.

Drawing upon an impressive array of primary sources from an archive only recently opened, Douglas Richmond offers a revisionist synthesis of the Carranza years of the Revolution. By thoughtfully assessing the nationalistic ideology and social programs of the Carranza era—agrarian reform, labor policy, progressive taxation, economic nationalism, and the doctrine of nonintervention—Professor Richmond rejects the notion that the First Chief was a political moderate. A more useful description, he holds, is that of "authoritarian populist." The social changes that occurred between 1914 and 1920 were lasting and significant as Carranza successfully challenged the old order.

How, then, does one explain Carranza's overthrow and assassination? Professor Richmond's answer is provocative. Carranza, as had some of his predecessors, found it impossible to reconcile the vastly divergent interests unleashed by the Revolution. As the second decade of the twentieth century approached he turned away from his own reformist impulse and, to make matters worse, selected an unpopular politician to succeed him in the presidency. For these indiscretions Carranza paid the supreme penalty in the hamlet of Tlaxcalantongo.

While to some compromise is an act of tremendous statesmanship, to others it is tantamount to weakness and the surrender of basic principles. Alvaro Obregón never indulged himself in the dialectics of this theoretical debate; but, as David Bailey forcefully demonstrates, he believed fully in the value of steering a middle course. A compromiser, Obregón saw as his task reconciling the vested interests of labor and capital, agrarianists and landowners, Catholics and anticlericals, and Mexican nationalists and the United States government. That he encountered some degree of success in this seemingly hopeless task, where so many before him had failed, was amazing; but, as Bailey perceptively indicates, the time was finally right. The violent decade from 1910 to

1920 had left an exhausted and despondent Mexico. Much as Mexicans in 1876 had been willing to accept even an excessive dictatorship in the interest of law and order, Mexicans in 1920 were prepared to embrace the politics of accommodation.

Although the Mexican Revolution was not a peasant revolution, abuse in the rural areas and the need for reform were recognized by every administration in the post-1910 period. As Lyle Brown indicates, however, it was not until the presidency of Lázaro Cárdenas (1934–1940) that agrarian reform figured prominently as an administrative goal. Slow progress on the agrarian front, Cárdenas contended, resulted in part from a lack of peasant unity. Therefore, he threw his personal prestige and that of his office behind the foundation of the CNC, the Confederación Nacional Campesina.

As Brown shows, the task was not an easy one because different groups within the country, most notably organized labor, recognized the political potential of a unified peasantry and sought to use the unification issue for sectarian ends. Ultimately, however, Cárdenas's own plan for unification carried the day, and the mobilization of the Mexican peasantry in the CNC helped him solidify his own position and enabled him to embark upon a series of social programs designed to alter the fabric of Mexican society.

Many historians contend that the Mexican Revolution died in 1940, when President Cárdenas turned over his office to his conservative successor, Manuel Avila Camacho. Whether the Revolution died or not the orientation certainly changed after 1940. Much had been done to vindicate the efforts of the rebels of 1910, but the intervening thirty years had already bequeathed a legacy of new problems. It was now time to reorder priorities and seek new solutions. The fighting was over; Mexican presidents would not again be driven from office before their terms expired. From the adversity of the second decade of the century, major accomplishments had followed; but those who had believed that the semifeudal society inherited by the Revolution would be replaced with socialism had to reexamine their expectations. By the end of World War II it was increasingly certain that the post-Cárdenas period would be typified not by socialism but instead by industrial capitalism.

If agrarianism represented the ideological antithesis of industrialization, it was the former that precipitated the latter. The agrarian reform program served to expand Mexico's domestic market and made it inviting to industrial capital. By carrying the Mexican Revolution to the left, Cárdenas inadvertently made Mexico's conception of modernity synonymous with the industrial state. The problem of the postwar period was clearly set: how to reconcile the needs for economic development with those of social justice. To articulate the problem was easy—to resolve it, hard.

Madero: The "Unknown" President and His Political Failure to Organize Rural Mexico

WILLIAM H. BEEZLEY

ELIAS MARTINEZ caused a sensation in his village when he decided to soar over the rooftops and off into the clouds above San José de Gracia. His effort to fly like a bird moved Luis González, the town's historian, to celebrate this local hero: "Elías had made himself a framework, with wings of grass matting. He strapped it on his back and climbed up into an ash tree. He called down to a friend standing below and asked him to frighten him out of the tree. His friend threw a rock at him, and Elías took wing. He was nearly killed, according to some, because he forgot to make himself a tail and beak; others said it was because his friend had not scared him enough."[1]

Coincidentally with Martínez's leap, Francisco Madero attempted the political reform of Mexico. This Coahuilan *hacendado* first tried an election campaign and then rebellion to overturn the dictatorship of Porfirio Díaz. As president in 1911, Madero returned to reform politics as a way to remake Mexican society; but just as Martínez's friend threw a rock at him in order to aid his flight, so rivals threw rocks at Madero's movement in order to smash it. On every side armed bands led by Bernardo Reyes; Pascual Orozco, Jr.; Félix Díaz; and Emiliano Zapata challenged the new president.

Madero's inability to reestablish peace undermined any chance of success for his programs and resulted in his assassination. His reform program failed.[2] Some cantina politicians claimed Madero's policies had been too moderate; others charged they had been too radical. Their remarks were the equivalent of saying that Madero "forgot to make himself a tail and beak" or that his friends "had not scared him enough."

Madero's rebellion and reform program were the most notable events in Mexico from 1910 to 1913, just as Martínez's flight was the most amazing event in San José de Gracia during those same years. Was there some relation between the failures of these two men? The question cannot be answered without first determining Madero's political apparatus and how he planned to get it into operation.

Madero entered politics in Coahuila's 1905 gubernatorial campaign[3] and then stepped into the national arena in 1908, joining the politicking in the 1910 presidential race. His efforts stayed well within the political environment established by Mexico's dictator of more than thirty years, Porfirio Díaz. In his political tract, *The Presidential Succession of 1910*, Madero celebrated the dictator's contributions to Mexican development, praising particularly the nation's economic progress since 1876. He argued, however, that Mexico faced eventual economic dislocation and social upheaval if the political system was not reformed.

The first problem, he pointed out, was that Mexico's leaders habitually remained in office. This practice, called *continuismo*, occurred even when regular elections were held because those in power controlled the electoral process. The second problem he identified was rigged elections.[4] Consequently, almost the only method of removing officeholders was by taking up arms—fighting that damaged the economy and disrupted society, destroying national progress.

Madero wanted to retain the best aspects of the Porfirian administration, sustaining economic growth and maintaining social stability. Madero summed up the solution in his slogan, "Effective Suffrage and No Reelection," which meant "A real vote and no boss rule." He called his political organization the Anti-reelectionist party. In the campaign that followed, Madero seldom commented on social and economic conditions in Mexico. For this reason he has been criticized as insensitive to what revolutionaries considered Mexico's serious problems, such as the land question.

Madero had no concern beyond political issues. He was a member of the emergent national bourgeoisie, a group that had little complaint with the economic system.[5] Moreover,

Madero believed that reform of social conditions was best left to local reformers. He rather blithely suggested that after the resolution of political problems, any necessary social and economic adjustments could easily be made by responsible, freely elected representatives. Beyond his call for honest elections and rotation in office, Madero planned a reversal of the trend to centralized control that had been the hallmark of the Díaz regime.

Porfirian centralization of authority had tightened after 1890, through the imposition of agents representing the national administration. Mexico City's proconsuls came in many guises. For example, clerks removed record-keeping duties from parish priests who had held them since the Spanish conquest. Other bureaucrats collected vital statistics that provided the national administration with information for the assessment of taxes and assignment of quotas for troop conscription. For rural Mexicans, compliance with laws requiring registration of births, marriages, and deaths often meant unnecessary—and sometimes expensive—journeys to offices located in district or state capitals. Other emissaries, such as census takers and tax collectors, came to the hinterlands; but the most visible—and the most hated—were the district prefects, called *jefes políticos*, and the *rurales*, or rural police.[6]

The appointment of district prefects meant substituting agents who answered only to the central government for locally chosen district administrators. The prefect destroyed the façade of local representative government and struck down one of the fundamental institutions of nineteenth century reformism, the *municipio libre*—the autonomous community.

What galled provincial Mexicans most was that the prefects replaced their own leaders. Almost without exception, the prefects were interlopers—either strangers to the district or outsiders to the political hierarchy. By creating a new and, therefore, suspicious pecking order, the appointment of prefects upset a social arrangement that had been firmly established in custom and honored in tradition.

Porfirian administrators, driven to secure their grasp on the nation, augmented the jurisdiction of these district prefects. Beginning as the political representative of the central government, the *jefe político*'s power was increased until it smothered local activities, wrecking the last remnants of authority remaining to local government.

Prefects received enhanced jurisdiction to regulate the economy by issuing licenses for local stores and peddlers, permits for the sale of alcoholic beverages, authority for the operation of toll roads and bridges, and so forth. They also received tremendous powers to enforce social control. They could, and did, dictate social standards in the community and district. Since the prefects were also free to fill their troop conscription quotas as they saw fit, malcontents, troublemakers, vagrants, and the prefect's rivals in commerce, politics, and love, found their way into the army, consigned there by the federal appointees.[7]

For the more difficult problems of social control the prefect could resort to the *rurales*. Mexico's rural police represented an organized, professional expression of the country's tradition of using special military units for social control. In the last years of the Spanish colony, Mexicans had formed the Acordada, a kind of vigilante force to deal with the bandits and vagrants that plagued the highways and the countryside.[8] The Acordada disappeared after independence and the number of highwaymen increased until Mexico earned a reputation as a bandits' roost.

Benito Juárez reacted to the problem in the same way as had other governmental leaders faced with outlaws in the rural areas. He initiated a constabulary that relied on mobile patrols of two or three men to maintain law and order in the widely scattered settlements. Juárez's rural police, although dressed differently, had much the same duties as the Texas Rangers and the Royal Canadian Mounted Police.

Díaz, in turn, used the rural force to extend his authority into the backlands—and perhaps to prevent the army from holding a monopoly of weapons. The dictator strengthened his *rurales* by leaving to their discretion the enforcement of law and order. Although the brutality of the *rurales* has certainly been exaggerated, they nonetheless exercised the *ley fuga* (the right to shoot to death escaping prisoners) with considerable casualness, and they most assuredly committed atrocities.[9]

Centralization came from the dictator's development of Mexico. With improved roads, newly constructed railroads, and the extension of telegraph lines, the national government seemed closer at hand. As modernization shrank the nation, it made the national government more visible and highlighted an unofficial agent of Mexico City, the foreign entrepreneur.[10] A fellow traveler of centralization, the foreigner held a position even more sacrosanct than the government agent. Although not subject to the national regime, the foreigner received protection from Díaz.

Strangers, representing or receiving the tutelage of the central government, arrived all over Mexico during the last two decades of the Porfirian age. Bureaucrats, *rurales*, and foreigners regulated politics, established social standards, controlled economic opportunities, and even altered the tempo of life. To be sure, the patterns of life in rural Mexico had never been freely determined; local elites had always dictated them. Abruptly, it was no longer one's patron, *compadre*, or acquaintance who guided village affairs. Thus, when Madero spoke out concerning specific political issues, he excited these less clearly and perhaps poorly understood grievances against infringements of local autonomy.

When Madero's revolt triumphed in the spring of 1911, he planned to roll back centralized authority by restoring autonomy to the states and communities. The Anti-reelectionists intended to redeem the 1857 Constitution, especially those articles which established a confederation. Each state's official seal and title included the word *sovereign*, and Madero and his followers intended to give meaning to this word. Their slogan, "A real vote and no boss rule," took aim at the "official" candidates and the bosses who rigged elections for the central government.

Madero planned to delegate to the state governors the responsibility and the opportunity to reconstruct Mexico. This delegation was no casual abdication of authority, but rather a carefully devised scheme of decentralization. It was consistent with his opposition to highly centralized government that had resulted from his heritage and his convictions. His birthright, as a son of remote Coahuila, the native state of federalism, included an abiding faith in confederated government. His philosophic precepts drew on Karl Christian Friedrich Krause and the Christian humanism movement that opposed the social homogenization of governmental consolidation. Overall, Madero opposed the society envisioned by Auguste Comte and promoted in Mexico by the positivists, the Científicos, and the dictator, because it was built on political consolidation.[11]

After his military victory in 1911, Madero and his Anti-reelectionist fellows called for the installation, as governors, of men who had been defeated by "official" Porfirian candidates during the most recent state elections. A cluster of motives dictated this decision. Some of Madero's closest allies had been unsuccessful gubernatorial aspirants. Other defeated candidates might also be enticed to the Anti-reelectionist cause by the opportunity to obtain office and by the promise to replace corrupt politics. Adherence to the Constitution had justified Madero's rebellion against the dictatorship.

Committed to state autonomy and confident that respect for regional aspirations would sustain him, Madero saw the governors as embodying a revolutionary appropriation of power. Consequently, he insisted on immediate replacement of several Porfirian governors, particularly those in Coahuila and Chihuahua, with men of *maderista* convictions. Urging his followers to restore vitality to state authority, the Anti-reelectionist leader presented the new governors with the difficult task of assuming power, of discharging rebel troops, and of restoring peace to the countryside. He also offered them the chance to initiate reforms that would represent his political program to state residents.[12] Madero was willing to entrust the fate of the Anti-reelectionist regime to the state governors.

Madero, in the first months after his military victory, demonstrated his commitment to state autonomy and his confidence that this ideology would sustain his authority. After signing the peace treaties of May 1911, Madero permitted Díaz to hand over authority to a caretaker government dominated by adherents to the old regime. Madero's presidential campaign and the voting would be supervised by the caretaker government.

Meanwhile, his political survival rested on his belief that the new governors could maintain order.[13] Madero allowed the governors to work out policies in local terms as long as the policies remained within the general guidelines of the Anti-reelectionist program established in the party platform and the *maderista* proclamation, the San Luis Potosí Plan. This policy had a certain rationality. Before the nationalizing experience of the Revolution, regions and localities had such different needs and desires that any national program became either a straitjacket that limited reforms or a nebulous system that lacked the potential to become a practical policy.

Madero recognized in his home state, for example, that "national problems, although common to all of Mexico, nevertheless, did not have equal importance in all the regions of the country. The agrarian problem, for example, was not so acute in Coahuila, with its great size and small population, as in the smaller, densely populated states. Neither did the incipient industry of Coahuila offer problems of such urgent solution as in the textile region of Veracruz and Puebla."[14]

The Madero experience, however, also demonstrated the weaknesses of using decentralized administration for the promotion of social reforms. Labor reforms, to be sure, required a strong commitment from the national government that could enforce the rules against powerful national and international companies. The implementation, not simply the institution, of reforms required the safeguards offered only by an active national government. The active state did not consolidate its role in Mexico until later, essentially not until the regime of Lázaro Cárdenas (1934–1940).

The failure of state autonomy, and along with it state government as an institution capable of carrying out reforms, resulted in part from the financial arrangement underpinning government in Mexico. The states and the localities simply did not have access to enough revenue with which to sustain major land, labor, or educational reforms. During the decade after 1910, the monies available to all levels of government were strikingly small. Beginning in the 1920s, however, there were increased numbers of pesos for reform. Of this income, the federal government took about 70 per cent, while the states and local administrations divided the remainder. For Madero to have made confederated administration successful would have required that he carry through an administrative and financial revolution—something he never considered.[15]

Because Madero only supported political changes and left it to the governors to initiate reforms, state administration offered a fertile seedbed of experience for later revolutionary leaders. Many of the men who would hold the nation's ministerial posts, serve as its presidents, and write the 1917 Constitution first sampled the exhilaration of attempting reforms and felt the frustration of working through bureaucracy as governors. The long list of onetime governors who advanced to national prominence includes Cárdenas, Plutarco Elías Calles, and Emilio Portes Gil, three governors who became president. Perhaps the most typical of these men who achieved national position was Carranza.[16] In any case, the Madero government tested decentralized administration, demonstrating its unworkable nature as a reform instrument. The governors were simply not enough.

Both Madero and Martínez the Birdman had relied on inadequate devices; but this statement does not answer the question: Were Martínez's unsuccessful flight and Madero's administrative failure both simple coincidences? An answer may be possible after an examination of Madero's appeal to the nation, that is, by looking at his attempts to mobilize Mexicans. Despite the fact that Madero had carried out intensive presidential campaigns, led a successful revolt, and initiated a program to restore local authority to state governors, Martínez—not Madero—was known in San José.

How typical were the residents of San José, who knew their local hero, Martínez, but knew nothing of their national leader? From the Federal District, the village of Milpa Alta is an example. This community of Nahuátl-speaking residents was only fourteen miles from the Zócalo, the central plaza of the capital city. Doña Luz Jiménez, who provided recollections of the revolutionary years in this village, remembered nothing of the Madero revolt; but she recalled the arrival of Zapata and his troops in the spring of 1911:

This was the first thing we heard of the Revolution. One day a great chief by the name of Zapata arrived from Morelos. He wore good clothes—a fine broad hat and spats. He was the first great man to speak to us Nahuátl. All his men were dressed in white—shirts, white pants, and they all wore sandals. All these men spoke Nahuátl more or less as we spoke it. Señor Zapata also spoke Nahuátl. When all these entered Milpa Alta, we understood what they said. Each of the Zapatistas carried pinned to his hat a picture of his favorite saint, so that the saint would protect him.

Zapata stood at the head of his men and addressed the people of Milpa Alta in the following way: "Come join me! I have risen in arms, and I have brought my countrymen with me. We don't want Our Father Díaz to watch over us any more. We want a better president to care for us. Join the Revolution with us since we are tired of the few cents the rich pay us. There isn't enough to eat or buy clothes. I want every man to have his own plot of land. He will sow it and reap corn, beans and other grains. What do you people say?"

"Will you join us?" Zapata asked the people of Milpa Alta and Señora Jiménez recollected that nobody answered. Some days later, the *zapatistas* went away.[17]

Other places around Mexico were also outside the events of the Madero adventure. Two more examples will suffice to illustrate the point. Pedro Martínez, the pseudonym of Oscar Lewis's informant in Tepoztlán, reported that the Revolution came to his village in 1911. He recalled: "The Revolutionaries entered Azteca [Tepoztlán] for the first time exactly on March 17, 1911. There weren't many of them, only about thirty, led by Lucio Moreno. They wore their *sombreros* on the back of their heads and held their muskets in their hands as they rode in. . . . They shouted 'Long live the Virgin of Guadalupe! Long live Francisco I. Madero!' and rushed to the *palacio* and began to burn it." This event meant little to Martínez as the rebel troops soon left his village with no recruits. Later, he summed up his memories of this phase of the Revolution by saying: "The Madero Revolution was almost over, and I still hadn't joined in the fighting. Madero was already president when Emiliano Zapata began to be heard of. It was in 1913 when his name was talked about, but we just criticized. Then you began to hear about Emiliano Zapata everywhere. It was Zapata this and Zapata that. But we said that he was only a peasant, not an intellectual man." Later, he concluded that Madero "became president but he didn't know what he was doing." Martínez did not join the fighting until 1914, when he enlisted with Zapata's armies fighting against Carranza's men from the north.[18]

From Chiapas comes another example. Juan Pérez Jolote, a Chamula Indian, knew nothing of the Revolution until 1913. While in a Tapachula jail, Pérez learned that President Madero had been murdered when two of his fellow prisoners asked to have their sentences commuted so that they could fight against their president's assassins. The jailer, accepting their proposal, decided to send all his prisoners to serve in the federal army. So Juan prepared to battle Madero's enemies and was promptly inducted into the army commanded by Victoriano Huerta—the man popularly accused of Madero's death.[19]

The military phase of Madero's revolt (1910–1911) was little known in Mexico's backlands. This phase of the Revolution covered only six months before the dictator resigned and went into exile, giving Madero an amazing victory. This reluctant rebel and his ragtag troops managed to win only a few battles in obscure places on the nation's outskirts. The insurrection did little more than call the dictator's hand and lead to the discovery that he had been ruling by bluff. The army and the *rurales*, because of corruption and inactivity, proved incapable of sustaining Díaz's authority.

Once Madero had launched his administration—at least when he had installed the caretaker government and ordered elections for national and state offices—it is indeed amazing that Mexicans knew so little about his activities. On the Gulf Coast, Andrés Iduarte recalled growing up in Tabasco and said of the Madero regime: "I detected no signs of it anywhere. The fact is that the Revolution . . . did not reach Tabasco until 1914."[20]

Since Madero placed such heavy emphasis on the governors during his assumption of power, they deserve a closer look. By June 15, 1911, the Anti-reelectionists had named provisional governors for each of the twenty-seven Mexican states, the Federal District, and the territory of Tepic. Of this list of officials, only eight eventually earned a place in Mexico's standard biographical directory, *Diccionario Porrúa.* The most notable were Venustiano Carranza, Abraham González, Alberto García Granados, and José María Pino Suárez. These were men in their late forties and fifties when they assumed office. Although certainly not young, they were younger by at least a decade than the men they were replacing.

Andrés Iduarte said of his state governor, "I do recall . . . Dr. Manuel Mestre Ghigliazza, the Maderista Governor of Tabasco. He was a poet, a physician, and a journalist; he was physically impressive and the idol of the children, who acclaimed him when he passed through our street mounted on a horse of imposing stature." Generally, however, the governors were men of unimposing natures. It seems probable that in most states the reaction of the people echoed Iduarte's first comment on the Revolution, that he "detected no signs of it anywhere."[21]

The simple fact is that Madero's Anti-reelectionist movement did not reach the simple and humble people of San José de Gracia and other villages like it. It must be admitted that the people of such villages were outside national life; but if the revolt were to accomplish anything, if Madero were to remain in power, he had to mobilize these rural villagers. What went wrong? How could Madero have mobilized people from the remote sections?

Two general networks reached into the countryside. First, there were such formal agents, usually outsiders, as foreigners and government agents, including tax collectors, law enforcement officers, and those in army garrisons. Villagers had a deep and understandable distrust of these outsiders, whether they happened to be Mexicans or not; and villagers usually accepted their leadership only when coerced or when under the threat of coercion. Second, there existed an informal network between the villagers and the greater world. This link was forged by priests, school teachers, itinerant peddlers, militia officers, and bandits. These persons were often natives of the village or they had deep roots in the local community through family relationships, longtime residence, or long acquaintance with the townspeople.[22]

The Anti-reelectionists in Chihuahua, for example, had access to the informal network into the western mountains and consequently had great success recruiting. Here Madero achieved his greatest military success. His principal organizers and military commanders were Abraham González, Pascual Orozco, and Pancho Villa. González, who had grown up in the city of Guerrero and lived there occasionally after becoming an adult, had kinfolk throughout the mountain districts. Orozco, a muleteer, was also from the mountains and had earned a reputation as an honest businessman and a trusted friend throughout the sierra. Villa, a cattle rustler, had a sympathetic reputation in the mountain villages where he often bartered protection, an odd meal, and a place to sleep in exchange for cash and goods smuggled from the United States.[23]

This informal network in Chihuahua was not duplicated or used elsewhere. Madero received tremendous criticism from other revolutionaries, and even more from later analysts of the revolt, because he attempted to do so little to capture the formal network with which to mobilize the people. His most concerted effort to create a patron-client system using relatives led only to exaggerated charges of nepotism.

Part of the president's problem was the makeup of his movement. The Mexican Revolution that began in 1910 was no more than a series of regional struggles. Certainly the sequence in which these local rebellions occurred was significant. Madero's insurrection in the north provided time and distraction for the *zapatista* movement to develop in Morelos, but the southern movement had little relation to the developments in Chihuahua. Zapata led an agrarian revolt—and agrarian rebellion had a heritage stretching back into the midnineteenth century. Earlier challenges to landlords and railroad companies had been smashed by the army and the *rurales*. Zapata's revolt probably would have been crushed except that the dictator's attention and troops were concentrated on Madero and the northern border. Mexico City could not devote its full military authority to smashing the Morelos *campesinos*.[24] Because of the regional differences in the revolutionary movement, Madero never commanded a disciplined, integrated rebel band or political party that could mobilize the nation's people.

Madero, moreover, failed to take control of formal networks into the backlands. He left the Porfirian bureaucracy essentially intact, maintained the Porfirian army, and continued the *rurales*, although incorporating a few rebel troops. The president discharged his army, except the few hundred troops merged with the *rurales*, and he snapped another political linkage by trying to abolish district prefects. The governors received little encouragement or guidance. They were free to develop or ignore connections with rural areas.[25]

Madero's only guidelines were that the governors restore peace, discharge rebel troops, and hold special elections for state and local offices. These instructions often worked at cross purposes. Restoring peace and discharging rebel troops simply were not possible in Morelos where, for example, halfway through the mustering-out process Zapata recognized that the government was not going to restore village lands immediately, if at all. He and his troops took back their weapons and returned to the field against the federal army, now representing President Madero. And so they remained until Zapata's assassination.[26]

Even when Madero decided to incorporate some loyal troops into the *rurales*, this incorporation did nothing to forge links to the people because he ordered these units garrisoned away from their native regions. This policy meant that the troops were unhappy about their relocation and that the residents of the area where they were stationed viewed them as merely another bunch of outsiders.[27]

The president's instructions that his provisional governors should arrange for state and local elections also did little to mobilize support for the new regime. In some states, despite Madero's appointment of provisional governors, there were contending politicians who fought among themselves for the right to be labeled as the official *maderista* candidate. When this rivalry matched men of reputation among the Anti-reelectionists, it disrupted necessary *maderista* unity.

This pattern, for example, occurred in Chihuahua where both Abraham González and Pascual Orozco sought nomination as the Anti-reelectionist candidate for governor in the summer of 1911. Madero was finally forced to intervene in the state's politics and called for Orozco to withdraw from the campaign. After less than a year of stewing over this slight, Orozco led an insurrection against Madero in March 1912, continued resistance to Madero's government, and eventually made an incredible alliance with Victoriano Huerta that endured until Orozco's death in 1915.[28]

Not only did rival Anti-reelectionist leaders battle for the spoils of Madero's military victory, but the revolt also provided an opportunity for those opponents who had been restrained by the dictatorship to resume their struggles, with one or both sides claiming to represent the Madero movement.

In Chiapas, the plaza politicians of San Cristóbal de las Casas and Tuxtla Gutiérrez seized on Madero's assumption of power as an opportunity to renew their struggle over the location of the state capital. The capital was located in San Cristóbal. Tuxtla's residents, led by the former Porfirian politician, Ramón Rebasa, insisted that the seat of government be changed from San Cristóbal "Chamula"—as Rebasa called the predominantly Indian town—to Tuxtla. During the summer of 1911, both cities put forward candidates for governor: Manuel Róvelo Argüello from Tuxtla and Policarpo Rueda from San Cristóbal.

When Tuxtla's residents managed to hold a rump meeting of the legislature and named their candidate as governor, San Cristóbal's leaders called for action. They organized volunteers to go to Tuxtla, prorogued the legislature, and placed their man in office. José Espinosa Torres, who organized San Cristóbal's volunteers, also enlisted a force of Chamula Indians into the expedition. Accusations back and forth as well as calls for federal intervention jammed the telegraph lines to Mexico City.

Both sides insisted that they represented the Anti-reelectionist cause in Chiapas. Tuxtla's leaders claimed that Bishop Francisco Orozco y Jiménez had cooperated in the mobilization of eleven thousand Chamulas and that the state was on the verge of an Indian uprising and a race war. From San Cristóbal came claims that the elections had been rigged and the capital relocated illegally. Both sides wanted federal troops. A distressed state citizen, Enrique Rau, wrote: "The state is in complete anarchy. The only solution is a declaration of a state siege and the appointment of a governor—with miltiary support. It is also essential that the governor not be from Tuxtla or San Cristóbal, but some neutral point, Comitán, for example." Bishop Orozco y Jiménez added that "the rivalry between the two towns has been great and extends far into the past, especially over the location of the state capital."[29] Madero's decentralized political policies had simply offered another opportunity for these old rivals to continue their longstanding contest for dominance in Chiapas.

Local struggles within the Anti-reelectionist movement, and between other regional groups, prevented Madero's administration from doing much about extending its reform into the countryside. Some governors did establish programs that went well beyond the vision of the national administration. These programs contained inventive reforms and were more successful at mobilizing the people than anything Madero proposed. The Madero government's effort at labor reform, for example, seemed feeble and ill conceived.[30] On the state level, however, individual governors secured legal changes that recognized unions, arbitration, and safety devices and resulted in higher wages, giving a new and more hopeful dimension to the worker's life. During the Madero years, some governors initiated dynamic, often dramatic, policies, for example in Chihuahua and Coahuila.

Abraham González took office June 2, 1911, in Chihuahua and won election to a full four-year term in August of the same year. Although publicly subscribing to the San Luis Potosí Plan, the governor ignored it to foster his own social and economic programs. González assumed the power to rule by decree and immediately revised the taxation system to encourage the redevelopment of commerce and industry disrupted by the fighting. He explained that he wanted to use taxes to force the division or increased productivity of large estates. He began regulation of previously tax-exempt corporations and ordered a plan of labor arbitration. González also announced his intention to eliminate company stores and successfully forced the closing of some. Failing to close others, he compelled store managers to sell goods at the same prices charged in the city of Chihuahua.

During the summer of 1911, González did not stop with legislation to better working conditions but sought to improve the daily lives of the state's workers. With motives that were more paternalistic than populist, he also wanted to control the evils that tempted workers. He tried to restrain alcoholism, extirpate gambling, and regulate vagrancy. While we may grant the moralistic nature of his programs, he went well beyond the politics of moral uplift to encourage education and was particularly eager to suppress the *jefes políticos* in favor of *municipios libres*. Governor González went so far as to seize company towns and declare them public settlements so that the residents could establish locally elected civil administrations.[31]

Venustiano Carranza carried out a parallel program of legislation in Coahuila. He attempted to return his state to Porfirian tranquillity by arming state guards to keep order, to prevent the molestation of large cotton estates in the Laguna district, and to protect the coal fields. These moves were made more to restore order than to favor the major businessmen who were usually foreigners.

Carranza also went to great lengths to collect information on the damages suffered by state residents in order to present these data to the national commission on indemnification. As governor, he introduced a new, steeply progressive taxation schedule. In his decree of the state's new *ley del catrastro*, he declared that the progressive taxes would force *hacendados* either to cultivate or to sell their fallow fields. He also initiated legislation to provide for such fundamental rights of workers as maximum weekly working days and daily hours, minimum salaries, insurance for accidents on the job, and arbitration of labor disputes.

Two other developments in Chihuahua appeared as well in Carranza's policies for Coahuila. Carranza extended paternalistic regulation of alcoholism and gambling to include other vices as well. He made an effort to curtail prostitution by prohibiting the entry of women into cantinas. He looked on the *municipio libre* as an essential political reform for the redemption of Mexico. His procedure, like that of González, was to eliminate the *jefes políticos* and to provide for freely elected municipal officials.[32]

The governors of both Chihuahua and Coahuila tried programs that went well beyond what Madero postulated in the San Luis Potosí Plan or attempted in his national administration. Both governors also developed their own formal and informal networks to garner support and to carry out reforms at the state level.

Carranza was particularly successful in mobilizing support. He sacrificed other reform programs to finance the costs of revamping the state's education system. An enormous sum, about 375,000 pesos, went for new schools, supplies, and the renovation of old buildings to be used by primary students. The state established nine night schools in the largest communities to teach basic literary skills to adults and applied pressure on industrial management to provide after-hours schools for workers. The normal school was enlarged to train more teachers, and an adjoining laboratory school opened for practice teaching.[33]

Teachers received special attention. The most common

complaint of Coahuila's teachers during the Porfirian years was that their salaries were frightfully low and payment irregular, often several months in arrears. Carranza ordered regular payment of salaries and called for wage increases so that incomes were improved by from 30 pesos to 50 pesos a month. In the larger cities, wages were even higher. These teachers represented an important network for Carranza.

Carranza and his followers attempted to invigorate local government by suppressing the symbol of dictatorial consolidation, the district prefect. In most districts he abolished prefectures, returning administration to locally chosen officials. These community politicians were assured that they had independence and the governor's support to devise programs that dealt with their community's needs.

Prefects were not the only threat to village governments. Large landholders and mining companies had also destroyed local autonomy through denunciations of land (including town commons) and by diversion of scarce water supplies. As a solution to this problem, the state government encouraged three policies: the incorporation of small mining and agricultural settlements to give them legal status and rights to land and water, the restoration of community lands that had usually been obtained by pressuring landowners to deed the property to the government, and the formulation of ways to share water by the enforcement of riparian codes and revised tax schedules.[34]

Carranza also wanted to maintain a state militia, despite Madero's order to discharge all rebel units by June 20, 1911. Carranza's concession to his men was a severance pay of 50 pesos for each veteran and an additional payment of 25 pesos for each weapon surrendered when mustering out. The payment of bonuses backfired as men took up arms again and received second, even third, payments for demobilization. Carranza ordered demobilization in Coahuila but tried to arrange immediate reenlistment, first into *rural* units and, after July 17, 1911, into state security forces. These latter units were stationed around Coahuila in small garrisons. Carranza considered this militia essential for maintaining himself in power.

Throughout his tenure, the governor had an intermittent argument with President Madero about the number, cost, and control of these troops. This quarreling halted only with the flare-up of military crises. Both the Reyes Rebellion of December 1911 and the insurgency of Orozco in March 1912 demonstrated to Carranza the need for state troops. The suppression of these military challenges to the government persuaded a short-sighted Madero that the state volunteers could be safely discharged. Militia units stationed in or near their home communities also served as an important link between the state capital and countryside, giving Carranza access to networks that Madero did not have and did not try to develop.[35]

Carranza's programs in Coahuila not only brought about political and economic reform, but also built a strong group of official and unofficial brokers who mobilized support for the governor. In March 1913, following the assassination of Madero, Carranza had the organization and the popular support to resist Victoriano Huerta's seizure of the presidency.

Madero directed the national administration from his inauguration in November 1911 until his overthrow in February 1913. During his brief fifteen months in office, he had little chance to learn from experience or to gain administrative skills. His policies, however, set the stage for his overthrow by threatening the vested interests that remained intact from the Porfirian years. The new president was a reformer and *hacendado* who favored Mexican development for the entire nation, rather than solely for the privileged few. He desired foreign investment but could not approve special tax and legal status for foreigners. He believed in the sanctity of property rights but could not countenance *hacendados* who persisted in seizing village lands and who often left land fallow. He endorsed the development of industry and expansion of transportation but would not permit exaggerated exploitation of workers to continue. He ignored the touchy sensibilities of the army's officer corps because he was a civilian who intended to restrict militarism in Mexico.[36]

Foreigners, *hacendados*, and entrepreneurs were willing to see Madero formed from office. The military provoked ten days of senseless killing of civilians and loyal *maderista* troops in Mexico City, which ended February 18, 1913, when Victoriano Huerta arrested Madero and his vice-president. The final act came after United States Ambassador Henry Lane

Wilson hastily washed his hands of responsibility for Madero's safety. Following orders given by the triumphant military commanders on the night of February 22, 1913, Maj. Francisco Cárdenas and Capt. Agustín Figueres shot to death Vice-President José María Pino Suárez and President Francisco I. Madero.[37]

Madero's assassination and the story of his martyrdom, spread by word of mouth, did more to politicize Mexicans than anything that he had attempted while alive. The mobilization of Mexico took place on a national scale for the first time since the crisis of the French intervention of the 1860s. Carranza and his followers began vigorously recruiting in the north, and soon Francisco Villa and Alvaro Obregón were rallying huge armies behind them. As the accounts from the villages of Milpa Alta and Tepoztlán reported, Zapata also began major recruitment in the south in 1913 and 1914. Huerta ordered massive conscription to fill his armies. The result was the militarization of Mexico, the mobilization of Mexicans as never before.[38]

More than coincidence linked Elías Martínez and Francisco Madero. That villagers in San José felt no relation to the events in Mexico City revealed that Madero had failed to reach rural Mexico. Only death extended his reach and gave him revolutionary stature.

Despite popular acclaim, Madero was no more than a silk-hat revolutionary. The label comes from an incident when Madero's troops occupied Torreón in late spring, 1911. Rebels began looting the town and celebrating their victory. By nightfall, they were marching in the streets. The leader of the parade had on a silk hat and was beating a commode resembling a drum. A bystander explained to the "drum major" how the commode was normally used. Immediately he threw it away in disgust, then marched on in his silk hat. Like this rebel, Madero was leading the Anti-reelectionists; but he opposed violence and social disorder. If he had known how revolution was normally used, he would have thrown it, like the commode, away in disgust and marched on in his silk hat.[39] Madero's leading a rebel military victory did not mean he could attempt a revolution in Mexico any more than Martínez's putting on wings meant he could fly.

In life, Madero was extremely short, with a high, whining voice, and given to idiosyncrasies, such as vegetarianism, that often made him the object of ridicule. In death, he became the David who had slain the Porfirian Goliath, a Christlike figure martyred for his people, the apostle of democracy. In death, the reformer became, in the popular mind, a revolutionary.

NOTES

1. Luis González, *San José de Gracia: Mexican Village in Transition*, trans. John Upton (Austin: University of Texas Press, 1974), p. 121.
2. The standard biographies of Madero are Charles C. Cumberland, *Mexican Revolution: Genesis under Madero* (Austin: University of Texas Press, 1952); Stanley R. Ross, *Francisco I. Madero, Apostle of Mexican Democracy* (New York: Columbia University Press, 1955); and José C. Valadés, *Imaginación y realidad de Francisco I. Madero*, 2 vols. (Mexico City: Antigua Librería Robredo, 1960).
3. Minutario Francisco I. Madero, Centro de Estudios de Historia de México, Fundación Cultural de Condumex, documentos núms. 67–83, carpeta 1, and núms. 84–165, carpeta 2, contain Madero's correspondence concerning the 1905 gubernatorial election in Coahuila.
4. Francisco I. Madero, *La sucesión presidencial en 1910* (San Pedro, Coahuila: privately printed, 1908).
5. Albert L. Michaels and Marvin Bernstein, "The Modernization of the Old Order: Organization and Periodization of Twentieth-Century Mexican History," in *Contemporary Mexico*, ed. James W. Wilkie, Michael C. Meyer, and Edna Monzón de Wilkie (Berkeley and Los Angeles: University of California Press, 1976), pp. 688–694.
6. Díaz's consolidation of power and efforts at centralization are traced in Daniel Cosío Villegas, *Historia moderna de México*, vol. 9, *El Porfiriato: La vida política interior*, Segunda Parte (Mexico City: Editorial Hermes, 1972). For a case study of government consolidation and its impact on local politics, see William H. Beezley, "Opportunity in Porfirian Mexico," *North Dakota Historical Quarterly* 40, no. 2 (Spring 1972): 30–40. Also see Michael C. Meyer, *Mexican Rebel: Pascual Orozco and the Mexican Revolution, 1910–1915* (Lincoln: University of Nebraska Press, 1967), pp. 14–15, 17. The legislation that reorganized rural Chihuahua, for example, was *Ley reglamentaria para la organización de los distritos del estado de Chihuahua* (Chihuahua: Imprenta del Gobierno, 1904).
7. The opposition to the prefecture, demands for its elimination, and

reestablishment of the *municipio libre* are found throughout the revolutionary literature, including the 1906 Plan of the Mexican Liberal party and the 1910 party platform of the Anti-reelectionists.

8. Colin M. Maclachlan, *Criminal Justice in Eighteenth Century Mexico: A Study of the Tribunal of the Acordada* (Berkeley and Los Angeles: University of California Press, 1974).

9. Paul Vanderwood, "Genesis of the Rurales: Mexico's Early Struggle for Public Security," *Hispanic American Historical Review* 50 (November 1970): 323–344; John W. Kitchens, "Some Considerations of the *Rurales* of Porfirian Mexico," *Journal of Inter-American Studies* 9, no. 3 (July 1967): 441–455; an accounting of atrocities committed by the *rurales* can be found in John Kenneth Turner, *Barbarous Mexico* (Austin: University of Texas Press, 1969).

10. Luis Nicolau D'Olwer, "Las inversiones extranjeras," in *Historia moderna de México*, ed. Daniel Cosío Villegas, vol. 7, *El Porfiriato: La vida económica*, Segunda Parte (Mexico City: Editorial Hermes, 1965), pp. 973–1177. An excellent study of foreign investment in one Mexican state and its relation to the strengthening of a powerful state elite is Mark Wasserman, "Oligarchy and Foreign Enterprise in Porfirian Chihuahua, 1876–1911" (Ph.D. diss., University of Chicago, 1975); also see Harold D. Sims, "Espejo de caciques: Los Terrazas de Chihuahua," *Historia Mexicana* 18, no. 71 (January–March 1969): 379–399, especially pp. 391–398.

11. William D. Raat, "Ideas and Society in Don Porfirio's Mexico," *The Americas* 30, no. 1 (July 1973): 32–53, especially pp. 50–53; Fredrick B. Pike, *Spanish America, 1900–1970: Tradition and Social Innovation* (New York: W. W. Norton, 1973), pp. 15–28.

12. For a general discussion of the governors during the Revolution, see William H. Beezley, "Research Possibilities in the Mexican Revolution: The Governorship," *The Americas* 29, no. 3 (January 1973): 308–313; an excellent case study of the fitful history of one of Madero's governors is Susan M. Deeds, "José María Maytorena and the Mexican Revolution in Sonora," *Arizona and the West* 18, no. 1 (Spring 1976): 21–40, and 18, no. 2 (Summer 1976): 125–148.

13. Manuscript sources for the provisional government are the Archivo Particular de Alfredo Robles Domínguez, Instituto Nacional de Estudios Históricos de la Revolución Mexicana; Archivo Madero, Correspondencia del Presidente Francisco I. Madero, Biblioteca Nacional (hereinafter cited as BN); and Manuscritos de Francisco León de la Barra, Centro de Estudios de Historia de México, Fundación Cultural de Condumex (hereinafter cited as Condumex/FLB).

14. José de la Luz Valadés, *Carranza (Refutáciones Históricas)*, Colección de Escritores Coahuilenses no. 16 (n.p., 1959), p. 52. All translations from Spanish in this essay are mine.

15. James W. Wilkie, *The Mexican Revolution: Federal Expenditure and Social Change* (Berkeley and Los Angeles: University of California Press, 1967), pp. 3, 11.
16. See Beezley, "The Governorship," pp. 308–311.
17. Luz Jiménez, *Life and Death in Milpa Alta: A Nahuátl Chronicle of Díaz and Zapata*, trans. and ed. Fernando Horcasitas (Norman: University of Oklahoma, 1972), pp. 23, 27.
18. Oscar Lewis, *Pedro Martínez: A Mexican Peasant and His Family* (New York: Random House, 1964), pp. 77–78, 87, 89.
19. Ricardo Pozas, *Juan, the Chamula: An Ethnological Re-creation of the Life of a Mexican Indian*, trans. Lysander Kemp (Berkeley and Los Angeles: University of California Press, 1969), p. 28.
20. Andrés Iduarte, *Niño: Child of the Revolution*, trans. James F. Shearer (New York: Praeger, 1971), p. 15.
21. Ibid., p. 16.
22. Eric R. Wolf, *Peasant Wars of the Twentieth Century* (New York: Harper & Row, 1969), p. xiii, and "Aspects of Group Relations in a Complex Society: Mexico," *American Anthropologist* 59 (1956): 1015–1078; Eric Hobsbawm, *Bandits* (New York: Dell, 1969), pp. 13–33, 83–93; James D. Cockcroft, "El maestro de primaría en la Revolución Mexicana," *Historia Mexicana* 16, no. 64 (April 1967): 565–587; David L. Raby, "Los maestros rurales y los conflictos sociales en México (1931–1940)," *Historia Mexicana* 18, no. 70 (October 1968): 190–226; and, chapters 6, 7, and 8 in Gilbert M. Joseph, "Revolution from Without: The Mexican Revolution in Yucatán, 1915–1940" (Ph.D. diss., Yale University, 1978).
23. William H. Beezley, *Insurgent Governor: Abraham González and the Mexican Revolution in Chihuahua* (Lincoln: University of Nebraska Press, 1973), pp. 13–54.
24. John Womack, Jr., *Zapata and the Mexican Revolution* (New York: Knopf, 1969), p. 66.
25. On the discharges, see Madero to Carranza, June 18, 1911, BN, box 1, núm. 340, and Peter Calvert, *Mexico* (New York: Praeger, 1973), p. 86. Also see Madero to Francisco León de la Barra, July 15, 1911, Condumex/FLB, carpeta 2.
26. Womack, *Zapata*, pp. 105–109.
27. Meyer, *Mexican Rebel*, pp. 41, 44.
28. Beezley, *Insurgent Governor*, pp. 71–88.
29. See the correspondence between representatives of the contending towns with the provisional president de la Barra in documentos núms. 131–153, carpeta 2, Condumex/FLB. Federal troops imposed a state of siege in Chiapas in September 1911. As late as 1915 the reverberations of this struggle, reminiscent of an Old West county-seat war, were still being reported. See Jefe de Hacienda to Carranza, April 9, 1915, Manuscritos de don Venustiano Carranza, Centro de Estudios de Historia de México, Fundación Cultural de Condumex.
30. Ramón Eduardo Ruiz, "Madero's Administration and Mexican

Labor," in *Contemporary Mexico*, ed. Wilkie, Meyer, and Wilkie, pp. 187–203; also Ruiz, *Labor and the Ambivalent Revolutionaries: Mexico, 1911–1923* (Baltimore: Johns Hopkins University Press, 1976).

31. González's reform program is reported in the state's official publication, *El Periódico Oficial*, from June to August 1911 and has been analyzed in Beezley, *Insurgent Governor*, pp. 55–114.
32. Carranza's program has been examined in William H. Beezley, "Governor Carranza and the Mexican Revolution in Coahuila," *The Americas* 33, no. 1 (July 1976): 50–61.
33. For a summary of Carranza's educational programs, see his statements to the state legislature, June 29, 1912, Archivo General del Estado de Coahuila, legajo 311, exp. Congreso (hereinafter cited as AGEC); on salaries see, as an example, legajo 306, exp. Saltillo, and *Periódico Oficial del Estado de Coahuila* 19, no. 46 (July 8, 1911): 2 (hereinafter cited as PO).
34. Carranza, circular núm. 124, January 6, 1912, AGEC, legajo 307. As an example of land cessions to restore villages lands see AGEC, legajo 303, exp. 11,1912; illustrative of the question of water rights is Andrés G. García to Carranza, October 3, 1911, AGEC, legajo 293, exp. 11,177. Also see Clifton B. Kroeber, "La cuestión del Nazas hasta 1913," *Historia Mexicana* 20 (January–March 1971): 412–427.
35. Efforts to recruit former rebels into state *rurales* are reported in Carranza's correspondence with the minister of internal affairs, AGEC, legajo 293, exp. 11,152; Roberto Rivas to governor, July 27, August 9, and November 17, 1911, AGEC, legajo 293, exp. 11,185; Carranza's efforts to arm his troops is reported in AGEC, legajo 293, exp. 11,174, and legajo 305, exp. 11,298. While the financing of these units is discussed in legajo 303, exp. 11,186, their activities can be followed in Pablo González's correspondence with Manuel Caballero, January 26, 1913, documento núm. 52, and with Antonio Rábago, January 27, 1913, documento núm. 54 in Manuscritos de Manuel W. González, Centro de Estudios de Historia de México, Fundación Cultural de Condumex, carpeta 2.
36. For an excellent summary of the Madero regime and the forces that brought him down, see Charles C. Cumberland, *Mexican Revolution: The Constitutionalist Years* (Austin: University of Texas Press, 1972), pp. 3–22.
37. The most thorough reconstruction and analysis of Madero's overthrow and assassination is found in Michael C. Meyer, *Huerta: A Political Portrait* (Lincoln: University of Nebraska Press, 1972), pp. 45–82.
38. Ibid., pp. 83–108.
39. Tulitas Jamieson, as told to Evelyn Payne, *Tulitas of Torreón: Reminiscences of Life in Mexico* (El Paso: Texas Western Press, 1969), p. 123.

Villa: Reform Governor of Chihuahua

FRIEDRICH KATZ

NEARLY seventy years after the outbreak of the Mexican Revolution in 1910, most of its leaders have found a resting place—both in history and in the official ideology of the Revolution.

There are, at times, contradictions between their roles in both of these worlds; but the controversies that these contradictions have sparked have taken place mainly among historians. Despite some discussions, there now exists a wide margin of agreement among scholars concerning Emiliano Zapata, Venustiano Carranza, and Alvaro Obregón. There is an exception to this rule, however. One personality—Francisco "Pancho" Villa—still evokes the most violent controversy and arouses the strongest feelings among historians as well as in a far broader spectrum of opinion.[1]

The emotions that Villa arouses may be gauged by the fact that, when his body was transferred in 1977 from a burial site in Durango to the Monument of the Revolution in Mexico City, thousands of people lined the streets of Parral in Chihuahua and shouted "Viva Villa" as Villa's remains were carried through the streets. These emotions may also be gauged by a book recently published in Mexico City that bears the suggestive title, *Villa, the Fifth Horseman of the Apocalypse.*[2]

The intense feelings that Villa still evokes are linked to his controversial personality; but the causes for the disarray and lack of consensus among historians and ideologists go much deeper. They are the result of a wide variety of factors.

For one thing, Villa does not fit into any convenient slot —he cannot be called a peasant revolutionary, a bourgeois revolutionary, or a working-class revolutionary. Zapata and Carranza left programs and plans—the Plan de Ayala for Zapata and the Constitution of 1917 for Carranza—that became rallying points for their supporters. For scholars, these programs and plans constituted a good base from which to assess these leaders' practical policies, although historians might now question to what degree these leaders were, in fact, applying their own programs.

Villa's legacy, by contrast, is not a plan or document. His legacy is a legend or, more accurately, a series of legends that have contributed to obscuring both the man and his movement. The question of whether a genuine social revolutionary existed under the legendary layers of a bandit, killer, gunman, womanizer, macho, and more has never really been answered because the practical policies he and his movement implemented while holding power in Chihuahua have never been examined. Nor has a related question ever been dealt with—the question of whether the Revolution in Chihuahua was similar to other rebellions in Mexico and what special characteristics it may have presented.

As more and more regional studies emerge, it is becoming increasingly clear that what is known as the Mexican Revolution of 1910–20 never was the general uprising and revolt it has so frequently been made out to be, most notably by Frank Tannenbaum in his remarkable book, *The Mexican Agrarian Revolution*.[3] Not one but, at least, four distinct revolutions took place during that period. Although their primary centers were in the state of Morelos and the northern states of Coahuila, Sonora, and Chihuahua, they had secondary ramifications in a series of other states.

In social and political terms, the revolutions in Coahuila and Morelos stood at opposite ends of a wide spectrum. The Coahuilan revolution, led by a wealthy *hacendado*—Francisco Madero—and supported by other important landowners in the state, was fought primarily to carry out political changes but not social changes. By contrast, the revolutionary movement in Morelos, led by Emiliano Zapata, was essentially a peasant movement. Having few, if any, links to other classes of society, its rallying cry was a demand for profound agrarian reforms.

The revolutions in Sonora and Chihuahua, in social

terms, stood somewhere between extremes in Coahuila and Morelos. In Sonora, an *hacendado*, José María Maytorena, led the revolt. In contrast to the situation in Coahuila, however, a much smaller group of landowners joined this movement. In economic and social terms, Maytorena and the landowners who supported him had far less power than Madero and his adherents. Unlike their counterparts in Coahuila, who were fighting for power on a national scale, the Maytorena faction had no ambitions beyond their home state of Sonora. Further, middle-class revolutionaries were more influential in the Sonoran revolution than in the Coahuilan.[4]

The revolutionary movement in Chihuahua was different from that in Sonora and Coahuila in that it was not led by *hacendados*, nor did any member of the landowning class ever occupy a prominent position in the leadership. It also was different from Zapata's movement in Morelos in that it was not led by peasants. Although peasant leaders played important roles in the lower echelons, it was not composed solely, or even predominantly, of members of the peasant class.

The insurgents from Chihuahua, in the main, consisted of a coalition of three different social classes. The leaders and most vocal supporters were members of the rapidly expanding urban and rural middle class in the state. The three most prominent spokesmen were Abraham González, political leader of the Revolution in the state from 1910 to 1911, who was a merchant, former rancher, and impoverished descendant of what had been one of Chihuahua's most powerful families; Pascual Orozco, the military leader, a relatively well-situated muleteer; and Silvestre Terrazas, the principal logician and intellectual supporter of the Revolution and the editor of the largest opposition newspaper, *El Correo de Chihuahua*.[5]

The reasons that induced this middle class to revolt were in some ways similar to those that led members of that same class to join the Revolution in many other parts of Mexico. Those reasons involved opposition to a dictatorship that restricted freedom and upward mobility in social, political, and economic terms and opposition to the ever-increasing influence of foreigners in all aspects of Mexican life.

In Chihuahua, a number of factors accentuated the dissatisfaction to a far greater degree than in many other parts of the country. The state was ruled by the wealthiest, most powerful, most close-knit regional financial and landowning group in all of Mexico—the Terrazas-Creel clan. Porfirio Díaz himself had feared this group and had prevented it from exercising political power in its native state. This separation of economic and political power in Chihuahua had given the rising middle class a certain leeway in both spheres. In 1903, however, Díaz reversed his attitude and gave the Terrazas-Creel oligarchy a monopoly in the political arena, which it combined with its already preeminent economic position. This change brought disastrous results for those members of Chihuahua's middle class who were not linked to the ruling oligarchy. New taxes were imposed upon them, and they all but lost any possibility of exercising, or participating in, any political power.

The large foreign—predominantly United States—investments in Chihuahua fueled nationalist resentment and discontent, and this feeling was compounded by the close ties foreign firms developed with the oligarchy. Foreign influence also made the state especially vulnerable to cyclical economic fluctuations. Chihuahua was hit harder than any other state in Mexico by the intense economic crisis of 1907, which originated in the United States. The effects of the 1907 crisis were reinforced both by the policies of the ruling group and by natural catastrophes. The oligarchy tried to shift the burden of the crisis onto the middle class by simultaneously calling in outstanding loans and raising taxes. In those same years a series of bad harvests caused food prices to soar.[6]

This same 1907 crisis affected large segments of the working class as well, especially miners and loggers who lost their employment by the thousands. Their ranks were swelled by thousands of unemployed Mexican workers who had worked in the United States and were forcibly repatriated to their homeland after they lost their jobs. These urban groups united with the local peasantry.

In some respects the peasantry of Chihuahua occupied a unique position in Mexico.[7] In the eighteenth century, the state had been the main target of attacks by roving Indian tribes, especially the Apaches. In order to counteract these attacks, the Spanish colonial administration had set up a number of military colonies located in strategic parts of the state, at such places as Cruces, Janos, and Namiquipa.

The members of the military colonies, whether Indian,

mestizo, or white, were granted extensive social, political, and economic privileges. In return for fighting the Apaches, they were given large grants of land and full municipal autonomy.[8] The number of these colonists and their rights increased after Mexico achieved its independence from Spain, since the Apache attacks now intensified. The state government and the wealthiest *hacendados*, such as the Terrazas family, continued their economic and military support of the military colonies.

With the defeat of the Indian tribes in 1885, the attitude of the *hacendados* toward the military colonists began to change. On the one hand, the colonists were no longer needed to ward off the attacks; on the other, their lands were becoming increasingly attractive to Chihuahua's great landowners after railroads linked the state to both the United States and central Mexico. Land values along the route of the Mexican Central Railway, which crossed Chihuahua from north to south, and the Chihuahua Pacific Railway, which passed through the western part of the state, rose sharply. The same was true of lands located near the border of the United States, where land values increased because of the economic development of the Southwest United States. Most of the military colonies had been established in these regions. From 1900 onward, the *hacendados*—at first with the tacit approval and, after 1904, with the enthusiastic support of the state government—did everything in their power to expropriate the lands of the colonists.

In 1903, Toribio Ortega, who headed the Junta Directiva de los Vecinos de Cuchillo Parado (a military colony that had been granted land by Benito Juárez in 1865), protested, in the name of 834 inhabitants, against a planned attack on the rights of the colony by a neighboring *hacendado*. "We know," he stated in a telegram to the federal Ministry of Development, "that Liceniado Carlos Muñoz is trying to obtain 10 *sitios de ganado mayor* belonging to the Colony of Cuchillo Parado. Since the documents he has in his possession were obtained by force, we ask you to discard his claims."[9] The villagers succeeded in warding off the attack; but the situation of the military colonies worsened greatly after the Terrazas-Creel clan assumed control of Chihuahua later that same year.

A special law was passed in 1905 by the Chihuahuan state legislature that facilitated the expropriation of these colonies. By 1908, some of the oldest and most prestigious of the colonies began to feel the effects of these measures. "We are deeply concerned about the fact that lands we consider our own, since we received them from our fathers and worked them with our hands, are now passing into other hands," the inhabitants of Namiquipa wrote to President Porfirio Díaz in that year; "If you do not grant us your protection, we will have to abandon our homes in order to subsist."[10]

Another of the oldest of the military colonies, Janos, sent an emissary, Porfirio Talamantes, directly to Mexico City. "The owners of the colony of Fernández Leal, located two leagues from Janos, are enjoying a comfortable life in the United States," he complained bitterly to Díaz, "while we, who suffered from the invasions of barbarians whom our fathers fought, cannot keep our own lands."[11]

Other colonies had a similar fate. Appeals for help to the national government were fruitless, and it is not surprising that these colonists played a key role in the Revolution of 1910. Toribio Ortega was the first revolutionary leader to rise against Porfirio Díaz in 1910. He later became one of Pancho Villa's most trusted generals. Porfirio Talamantes, the spokesman for Janos, also participated in the Revolution and became a colonel in Villa's army. The village of Namiquipa was a center of revolutionary activity in Chihuahua from 1910 to 1920. When Villa attacked Columbus, New Mexico, in 1916 a large part of his striking force was composed of inhabitants of Namiquipa.

Pancho Villa, who joined the Revolution in 1910, was at first just a local leader of the insurgent movement in Chihuahua. He was a man with a wide-ranging background—hacienda peon, miner, bandit, merchant—much of it shrouded in legend. The story that he was forced into banditry after killing an *hacendado* who had raped his sister is still disputed.

His record as a cattle rustler is not. Among a large segment of Chihuahua's prerevolutionary population rustling was not considered disreputable. Up to 1885, everyone had had access to the large herds of cattle grazing on the state's immense public lands. After the Apache wars ceased and railroads linked this northern state to both the United States and the rest of Mexico, the *hacendados* began exporting cattle and appropriating public lands. The people's traditional right to round up and sell wild cattle was abolished. Consequently, in the eyes of many Chihuahuan peasants, Villa was simply exercising rights that once had been theirs.

Cattle rustling, though, did not constitute the only link between Villa and the militant peasantry of northern Mexico. In the years before the outbreak of the Revolution, he had established his headquarters in the town of San Andrés, one of Chihuahua's oldest military colonies, which was involved in a protracted land and tax dispute with the state government. In 1908, the town had risen up against taxes imposed by the state.[12] This uprising, in which Villa did not participate, was put down by the state's authorities; but many of the veterans of that uprising joined Villa two years later when he took up arms in support of Madero.

In spite of these links with the village communities, Villa was not a traditional peasant leader like Emiliano Zapata in the southern state of Morelos. Many of the men who joined Villa—associates from his bandit days like Tomás Urbina, hacienda administrators like Nicolás Fernández, and foremen of cattle ranches like Fidel Avila—can scarcely be described as peasants.

Unlike Zapata, whose rise to preeminence was due, in large degree, to his political activity as spokesman for the peasants of Morelos, Villa's rise from a local to a state leader of the Madero movement was related exclusively to his extraordinary military capacities. His talent was as a guerrilla fighter and in his ability to mobilize and lead men. Also, unlike Zapata, Villa never drafted a political program or spoke out on social and other problems during the Madero revolution or during Madero's term as president of Mexico.

After Madero discharged Villa in 1911, and gave him 50,000 pesos and granted him amnesty, it appeared that Villa would return to private life. He bought a home in the city of Chihuahua and set up a butchering and meat-packing business. Nevertheless, he soon was drawn back into the political and social conflicts that engulfed Chihuahua after Madero's victory.

Without *hacendados* leading the revolutionary movement—or even participating in it—Chihuahua became the only one of the three northern states that had revolutionary administrations in which a non-*hacendado*, such as Abraham González, could become governor. The governors of the two neighboring states, José María Maytorena in Sonora and Venustiano Carranza in Coahuila, were *hacendados*. Unlike his counterparts who tried to spare their own class, González began to impose new taxes on the state's oligarchy. He refused, however, to expropriate the lands of the large landowners in favor of the peasants or even to return to former military colonists the lands that had been taken from them.

The result of González's activities was an unlikely alliance between Chihuahua's former ruling elite and revolutionaries who were disillusioned by Madero's and González's lack of reform; each believed it could use the other group for its own ends. The former military leader of the Revolution in Chihuahua, Pascual Orozco, whose gubernatorial ambitions Madero had refused to support, led this heterogeneous coalition against the Madero government.

Villa heeded the appeals of both the state and central governments and took up arms against his erstwhile commander, Orozco. Villa soon joined forces with federal troops under the command of Victoriano Huerta who had been sent north by Madero to put down the uprising. Huerta, who, until February 1913, insisted he was loyal to Madero, had served for years in the Porfirian army. Ever since the victory of the Revolution, he had systematically attempted to destroy the military forces that the Revolution had produced. In 1911 and 1912, he had provoked an armed conflict with Zapata in Morelos and had then proceeded to carry out a search-and-destroy operation against the southern guerrilla leader.

In 1912, Huerta applied the same tactics against Villa, who nominally was his ally and subordinate. He accused Villa of insubordination, dispersed his forces, and tried to have the Chihuahuan revolutionary shot. Villa was reprieved at the last moment by Madero, who suspended the impending execution; but, instead of freeing Villa, Madero had him transferred to a military prison in Mexico City. It was there that Villa met Gildardo Magaña, one of Zapata's lieutenants. It was Magaña who broadened Villa's vision of Mexico's problems, explaining to him the agrarian situation in the southern part of the country and the causes for the Zapata revolt.

Villa escaped from the military prison of Santiago Tlatelolco in November 1912. He succeeded in making his way to El Paso, Texas, where he remained as an exile. In March 1913, after the murder of Madero and Huerta's military coup, Villa crossed the Rio Grande with only eight men and again led a revolutionary movement in Chihuahua. His military successes were such that by December 1913 he had won control of the entire state and was leading an army of between five and ten thousand men, calling itself the Division of the North.

When the military commanders of the Revolution elected Villa governor of Chihuahua in December 1913, this semiliterate former peon suddenly found himself in a situation he had never before faced. Independent of all other variables, the administration of a large and rich state, with a complex economy largely geared to exports, would be difficult enough; but, besides the normal tasks of administration, Villa had to raise and finance an army capable of defeating Huerta. He had to set up some mechanism through which local leaders and local guerrilla bands, not all integrated into a broader movement, could be brought under his control.

At the same time that he was imposing on his state the tremendous burden of carrying out the war against Huerta, Villa had to win over to his side large sectors of the population who had supported Orozco or had joined Huerta. In a state with a long common border with the United States, huge North American investments, and a populace that had developed strong anti-United States nationalist tendencies, Villa had to maintain a precarious equilibrium. He had to retain, on the one hand, the goodwill of the United States government and North American companies in order to acquire arms across the border; but, on the other hand, he dared not alienate the nationalist segments of Mexico's population.

Villa had no organized political party or large group of intellectuals and experienced administrators on which he could rely to help him carry out the difficult tasks with which he was confronted. He was forced to devise an original system to solve these problems, since he could not, and would not, apply to his state the solutions that the leaders of other main factions in the field—Zapata and Carranza—were implementing in the territories under their control. Zapata's solution was to confiscate the large estates and return usurped lands to the peasant villages. This policy resulted in a great decrease in the production of cash crops, mainly sugar, because peasants used the restored lands mainly for subsistence production. The policy that Carranza was attempting to implement, though not always with success, was to maintain the social status quo as nearly as possible and to finance the Revolution by increasing taxes.

In Chihuahua, unlike Morelos, only a minority of the population consisted of peasants. Large-scale land redistribution, therefore, would not have gained Villa the support of the mainly nonagricultural inhabitants. Furthermore, it might have deprived him not only of the means to feed the urban unemployed, but also of the resources with which to finance his army. It was through the sale of cattle and agricultural products, mainly cotton, that Villa was able to obtain sufficient arms from the United States in order to maintain his famous Division of the North. Zapata, who had no common border with the United States, did not have the option of exchanging cash crops and cattle for arms. Carranza, himself a *hacendado* who enjoyed the support of a large segment of the large estate owners in Coahuila and Sonora, wished to maintain unchanged their social status—a policy Villa was neither willing nor able to follow.

The Chihuahuan oligarchy was the first in the country to attempt a counterrevolution. No revolutionary government could have survived in that state without destroying both the economic and political power of that traditional ruling class. Above all, if Villa wanted to gain the support of the lower classes who had become profoundly disillusioned by Madero's failure to implement the promises of social reform inherent in the Plan of San Luis Potosí, he had to go further than making vague promises of land reform.

Villa developed a highly sophisticated and extremely effective strategy for dealing with these problems. The cornerstone of this strategy was a decree he issued after becoming governor of Chihuahua. This decree of December 1913 ordered the confiscation of the land and other properties belonging to the wealthiest and most powerful Mexican land owners in Chihuahua, the most prominent of whom were the Terrazas, Creel, Cuilty, and Falomir families.[13]

In the short run, the profits from operating these haciendas were destined for the public treasury, which really meant to the army, and to pay pensions to the widows and orphans of soldiers who died during the Revolution. In the long run, after the victory of the Revolution, laws were to be passed that would completely and fundamentally change the ownership of these lands. A part was to be divided among the revolutionary veterans, another part was to be returned to former owners from whom the *hacendados* had taken them, while a third part was to remain at the disposal of the state, with the primary aim of paying for the widows' and orphans' pensions. Until the final victory of the Revolution, these lands were to be administered by the State Bank of Chihuahua.

Villa's measures had far-reaching consequences in military, economic, and social terms. The resources that the confiscated estates generated were used, for the most part, to equip and finance the army. As a result, the Division of the North became the most effective striking force of the Revolution and played a decisive role in the defeat of Huerta.

Another consequence of these confiscations was to give Villa the financial means to bind local guerrilla bands and their leaders to his army and to exercise effective control over them. Not only did Villa hold the purse strings, but, above all, he also was able to give or withhold arms at will. This economic power, together with his charismatic personality, welded into a coherent whole the very divergent groups of which his Division of the North was composed. The decree was even more important in social terms. It destroyed the power bases of the traditional oligarchy, which had played a major role in opposing the Revolution in Chihuahua.

Although Villa only promised but did not distribute land to the peasantry, he did succeed in gaining large-scale support within this class of society. This support might seem surprising, since Chihuahua's peasants were wary of promises. Madero had promised land; but, after assuming power, he did nothing for them. Villa's promises, however, were more convincing. His social origins may have impressed the peasants; but, mainly, his credibility was enhanced by the fact that he had confiscated the largest haciendas in the state and had expelled the landowners from Chihuahua. An additional factor was the establishment of a state agricultural bank to provide the peasants with credit.

There was an element of tradition that made the Chihuahuan peasants ready to accept some postponements of land distribution. The ownership of land by military colonists had always been linked to the obligation to "earn" it by fighting. In their eyes it was thus quite appropriate that land division should be linked to service in the revolutionary army. Villa's promise to give land to revolutionary veterans reinforced this attitude. Soldiers in the field would object strongly to agrarian reforms being carried out before they returned from the war. In addition Villa's decree also gained him the support of the urban poor, since much of the revenue from confiscated estates was redistributed to them.

Another decree issued by Villa as governor drastically reduced the price of meat. "The price of meat in Chihuahua is fixed at 15 cents, Mexican money, a kilogram instead of one peso formerly charged in federal reign," according to the *El Paso Times*. "The Government is operating the meat market and each day a detachment of soldiers is sent out to one of the Terrazas ranches and a herd of cattle is rounded up and brought into the city and slaughtered. The meat is then distributed to the various markets in the city."[14] A few weeks later the same newspaper reported: "Unemployed Mexicans of the devastated lumber camps and mines are being given daily rations. . . . Madera, Pearson, and Casas Grandes are daily provided with rations by the Constitutionalist Army. Townspeople are unable to secure employment because of the closing down of industries caused by the Revolution. . . . They call at the Constitutionalist Army Commissary and are provisioned under arrangements made by Villa, and the Constitutionalist Army bears the whole expense of providing for these people."[15]

Villa's measures benefited the poor and unemployed in yet another way. Thanks to the resources he now had with which to pay and equip his troops, thousands of Chihuahuans joined the army. As a result, despite the fact that many enterprises had closed down because of revolutionary turmoil, unemployment was drastically reduced in his state.

The middle class was less directly affected by these measures, except for those of its members who were officers in Villa's army or had become administrators of confiscated estates. Nevertheless, Villa did gain substantial support among his class. Many appreciated the order he imposed upon Chihuahua and, even more, they hoped to partake of national power once Villa gained supremacy in Mexico.

One group that looked, at first glance, like a very unlikely beneficiary of Villa's rule was the large North American community in Chihuahua. United States citizens, nevertheless, had substantial grounds to be happy with his rule. He neither confiscated their holdings nor greatly increased the taxes they were required to pay. Since revenues from confiscated Mexican estates provided him with sufficient income to meet a large part of his needs, at least until mid-1914, Villa did not want to antagonize the United States on which he had become increasingly dependent for the purchase of arms and supplies for his army. This policy of Villa's contrasted sharply with that of Carranza, who did not want to confiscate the estates of Mexico's oligarchy and was trying to shift the burden of financing the Revolution to foreign interests.[16] As a result, both U.S. companies and their government favored Villa over Carranza.

One of the main problems Villa faced in implementing his strategy was how to administer the confiscated properties, which included not only large landed estates but also banks, industrial plants, houses, and a wide variety of lesser enterprises. These administrative problems were of enormous magnitude, and Villa had no experience in administration. Most of the bureaucracy in Chihuahua had sided with Huerta. Villa had no political organization and few intellectual supporters; and there was a long and endemic tradition of corruption in Mexican history. How, then, could Villa prevent most of the newly acquired resources from being stolen or simply wasted?

His strategy was relatively simple but, on the whole, quite effective. The confiscated properties were divided into two parts. One part was turned over to the generals of the Division of the North. Villa made no attempt at direct control over their holdings. Some of the generals, such as Tomás Urbina, an associate from bandit days, could and did pocket some of the proceeds for themselves.[17] Nevertheless, Villa exercised a form of indirect control over the properties administered by his commanders—they were required to equip and outfit from the proceeds a large number of troops to fight in the ranks of the Division of the North.

The other part of the properties, the larger of the two, came under the administration of the state government. After several months of experimentation, Villa created the Administración General de Bienes Confiscados, at the head of which he placed one of his few intellectual supporters, Silvestre Terrazas, who had had some administrative experience and had been a newspaper publisher for many years.[18]

Many of the administrators continued to exercise their customary functions on the haciendas, only this time on behalf of the state. An effective means Villa had of ensuring their honesty was revolutionary terror. Even the faintest suspicion of theft could mean a firing squad. It may be said that Villa's administrators became extremely cautious and punctilious, though not always honest. On the whole, Villa never eliminated corruption or waste, but his system allowed him to obtain enough resources to implement both his military and civilian aims.

Revenues from the estates were supplemented by another form of "income"—paper money that Villa printed at an increasing rate. The printing of large amounts of paper currency has frequently been attributed to Villa's lack of comprehension of economics, since inflationary currency was apparently counterproductive for his economic aims.

Until Villa's defeat at Celaya, the value of his money, while steadily falling, did not depreciate commensurate with the amounts he was printing. The main reason was that foreign companies, as well as American and Mexican speculators, were acquiring and keeping large amounts of the currency. These speculators confidently hoped that it would become legal tender for all of Mexico because they believed that Villa could gain control of the whole country. By distributing large amounts of this money, both to his supporters and to the population at large, Villa broadened the base of his support even more.

What emerges from this description is a far more complex picture of the Villa administration in Chihuahua than has generally been assumed before. This picture is borne out by the impressions of observers who either lived through Villa's administration or visited Chihuahua during his rule. Patrick O'Hea was the British consul in Torreón, a hacienda administrator, and a man closely linked to the prerevolutionary oligarchy of the Laguna region in which he lived. It is no surprise that he was extremely hostile to Villa; yet, he wrote in his memoirs, "If, therefore, I am asked for a definition of the man, Pancho Villa, my reply can only be 'Which one?' for the man underwent the mutations of his own process of success or failure." "Multiply these," O'Hea continued, with grudging admiration, "by his fierce reaction against restraints, his savage reprisals against his enemies, the unspeakably undesirable character of his background friends, yet the excellent quality of some of his military and civilian advisers, his benevolence toward the poor, his unsleeping suspicions, his occasionally naive candor, and you will perhaps discover the man as I never could."[19]

Alden Buell Case was a Protestant missionary who experienced most of Villa's rule in Chihuahua. He summarized his impressions of Villa by saying,

> He was of lowly origin; he was without education; he was said to have been a bandit; his moral character was unworthy. But he was a man of extraordinary force, a military genius. He was popular, ardently admired by his followers, and even by his enemies, who regarded him with almost superstitious fear. After Villa had quarreled with Carranza and established his own authorities as supreme in the northern states, he showed no little political ability in associating himself with extremely capable men and organizing, insofar as conditions permitted, a beneficent government. He was doubtless honest in purpose to correct abuses and permit the permanent welfare of the people.[20]

Clarence Barrows, dean of the Graduate School of the Social Sciences at the University of California at Berkeley, who later became chancellor of that university, traveled to Chihuahua in the spring of 1915. It was a very extensive trip. "Barring a few days in Mexico City," Barrows recalled,

> I lived as the Mexicans are living in these present hard times, ate their beef, tortillas, and frijoles, slept with them about their fires in the pine forests of the Sierra Madre and on the mud floors of their ranchos. I rode with soldiers on the top of freight cars and with horses and mules across the great plains and hills.
>
> On the basis of the experience, I found the state of Chihuahua well-governed by the forces of Villa. I had anticipated anarchic conditions in places but found the contrary. . . . The Villa government has shown much ability in utilizing its resources. The Mexi-

can Central Railroad line is in good condition. . . . Telegraph and telephone lines have been repaired and extended; a new water supply for Chihuahua City restored; a mint established with locally devised machinery. Commissions are at work on new laws of finance, agriculture, labor, and land. I have their reports and, while they do not impress me for their thoroughness, they do reveal just and moderate ideas of reform. The schools are in operation and full of children. Villa, while an illiterate man, has given a strong impulse to instruction.

About Villa himself, Barrows concluded, "All who have seen him in recent months praise his growth in experience and moderation. His power lies in his splendid courage and audacity, his understanding of the Mexican lower classes, and a native shrewdness and common sense. In my opinion he is the most temperate and reasonable leader in Mexico."[21]

This description, as well as the accounts of eyewitnesses, should put an end to some of the myths concerning *villista* rule in Chihuahua. It was not a regime of cutthroats and bandits, characterized by an indiscriminate orgy of murder and plunder. While extortion and killing did take place in Chihuahua, as in all of Mexico during the Revolution, the scope seems to have been far more limited in that state than in most of the country, and to have been directed far more exclusively at the domestic upper class.

Villa's policies in Chihuahua represented a compromise between his desire for a large-scale redistribution of property and the practical necessities of winning a war and gaining a broad measure of support. On the whole, his policies were very successful both in Chihuahua and in the other regions of northern Mexico that he administered. He carried out a greater redistribution of income than any other leader except Zapata. The quality of his administration gained him the support not only of the poorest classes of society but also of large segments of the middle class of Chihuahua and of "revolutionary" *hacendados* of neighboring states. What is more, Villa's Division of the North was the decisive force in the defeat of the Huerta regime.

It goes beyond the scope of this paper to analyze the reasons why Villa, so successful in his struggle with Huerta, failed only a year later in his conflict with Carranza and Obregón. It may nevertheless be useful to offer some hypotheses. There are, for example, strong indications that the successful financial measures Villa undertook in Chihuahua contained the seeds of his defeat in the fight for power on a national scale. Issuing large amounts of paper money made him extremely vulnerable to the maneuvers of speculators. Their power made itself felt after Villa's first military defeat at Celaya. The speculators who had bought his money while counting on his victory, now dumped it at whatever the market would bear. The result was an enormous depreciation of his money. The ensuing inflation and food shortages seriously undermined his popular support.

Another possible explanation is that generals who administered some of the confiscated estates and many of the former administrators who had retained their positions and formed the conservative wing of the Villa movement and were more and more opposed to social change also contributed to Villa's loss of support. Villa's policy of delaying agrarian reform until his final victory, which had been accepted by the peasants of Chihuahua for personal and historical reasons, may have cost him the allegiance of large groups of the peasantry outside of his home state.

It is clear that Pancho Villa does not fit into any of the unidimensional molds into which he has been placed. He was not a single-minded bandit and plunderer, as he is so frequently depicted, whose regime represented one long nightmare for the people of Chihuahua. Neither, though, was he the single-minded agrarian reformer other historians have called him. In a society where peasants were a minority of the population, agrarian reform alone would not have solved the problems of the poor. Villa was—and there is, on the basis of his record in Chihuahua, no reason to doubt this—a genuine social reformer who had made a large-scale attempt to redistribute the wealth of the rich to the poor.

It is not surprising that he finally failed in his endeavors. He had neither the organization nor the technical or intellectual knowledge to reform society completely. In view of Mexico's proximity to the United States and the constraints put on the country by its geographical location, it is doubtful whether anyone, during two short years in power, could have carried out such profound reforms. What is surprising about Villa's administration of Chihuahua in the two years that his forces controlled the state are not his failures but his successes.

He was under tremendous constraints: he had to set in

motion an economy devastated by two years of revolution and civil war in Chihuahua. The problems he faced were enormous. In the first year of his rule he had to conciliate Carranza whose opposition was formidable. For the whole period that he ruled Chihuahua he had to conciliate the United States on whose arms and economic help he depended. The greatest constraint, though, was the need to wage offensive warfare against Huerta and to mobilize all the resources of his state for that purpose. Economies far more advanced than that of Chihuahua—and with more effective political organizations and first-rate economists—have failed in such endeavors. Villa, who had little technical competence, no effective political organization at his disposal, and very few highly trained intellectuals, managed, nevertheless, for a relatively long time to conciliate these aims. At the same time that he set up the most effective and best organized military organization that Mexico had known till then, he managed to effect a real and far-reaching redistribution of income and gained support among the most divergent social classes within his state.

At the height of his power, not only the poorer classes on whose adherence he could count until his death, but the highly vocal and developed middle class had also to a large degree given him their support. One of the means through which Villa managed to gain this large popular base was a policy of conciliation and restraint in repression, which contrasts strangely with the public image he has had for such a long time.

What has made Villa's administration and leadership so difficult to diagnose and to put into a convenient slot is that it was a complex mixture of at least five elements. Villa was, at one and the same time, a social bandit, a peasant leader, a traditional caudillo, a charismatic spokesman for the poor, and an administrator with at least some traits of a modern manager.

NOTES

1. The two extreme opinions about Villa are expressed most clearly, on the one hand, by ardent admirer Nellie Campobello, *Apuntes sobre la vida militar de Francisco Villa* (Mexico City, 1940),

and, on the other, by no less ardent enemy Celia Herrera, *Francisco Villa, ante la historia* (Mexico City: Editorial Libros de México, 1964).

2. Rodrigo Alonso Cortés, *Francisco Villa: El quinto jinete del Apocalipsis* (Mexico City: Editorial Diana, 1972).
3. Frank Tannenbaum, *The Mexican Agrarian Revolution* (New York: Macmillan, 1929).
4. For the best description and analysis of the Mexican Revolution in Sonora, see Héctor Aguilar Camín, *La frontera nómada: Sonora y la revolución mexicana* (Mexico City: Siglo Veintiuno, 1977).
5. See Robert Lynn Sandels, "Silvestre Terrazas: The Press and the Origins of the Mexican Revolution in Chihuahua" (Ph.D. diss., University of Oregon, 1962).
6. The Terrazas rule in Chihuahua is best described in Mark Wasserman, "Oligarchy and Foreign Enterprise in Chihuahua" (Ph.D. diss., University of Chicago, 1975).
7. See Friedrich Katz, "Peasants in the Mexican Revolution of 1910," in *Forging Nations: A Comparative View of Rural Ferment and Revolt*, ed. Joseph Spielberg and Scott Whiteford (East Lansing: Michigan State University Press, 1976), pp. 61–85.
8. Ibid.
9. Departamento Agrario, Mexico City, Dirección de Terrenos Nacionales Diversos, exp. 37x5, Junta of Cuchillo Parado citizens to Secretary of Development Ministry, January 10, 1903. All translations from Spanish in this essay are mine.
10. Departamento Agrario, Mexico City, Dirección de Terrenos Nacionales Diversos, exp. 178, letter of the inhabitants of Namiquipa to President Díaz, July 20, 1908.
11. Departamento Agrario, Mexico City, Dirección de Terrenos Nacionales Diversos, exp. 75–1407, letter of Porfirio Talamantes, representing the inhabitants of Janos, to President Díaz, August 22, 1908.
12. Francisco Almada, *La revolución en el estado de Chihuahua*, 2 vols. (Mexico City: Biblioteca del Instituto Nacional de Estudios Históricos de la Revolución, 1964), 2:65.
13. Friedrich Katz, "Agrarian Changes in Northern Mexico in the Period of *Villista* Rule, 1913–1915," in *Contemporary Mexico*, ed. James W. Wilkie, Michael C. Meyer, and Edna Monzón de Wilkie (Berkeley and Los Angeles: University of California Press, 1976), pp. 259–273.
14. *El Paso Times*, December 27, 1913. See also Almada, *La revolución*, 2:65.
15. *El Paso Times*, January 17, 1914.
16. Friedrich Katz, "Pancho Villa and the Attack on Columbus, New Mexico," *The American Historical Review* 83 (February 1978): 101–130.
17. John Reed, *Insurgent Mexico* (New York: International, 1969), p. 26.
18. Katz, "Agrarian Changes."

19. Patrick O'Hea, *Reminiscences of the Mexican Revolution* (Mexico City: Editorial Fournier, 1966), p. 160.
20. Alden Buell Case, *Thirty Years with the Mexicans* (New York: Fleming H. Revell, 1917), p. 176.
21. U.S. State Department Files 812.00, Clarence Barrows to I. Wheeler, July 25, 1915.

Carranza: The Authoritarian Populist as Nationalist President

DOUGLAS W. RICHMOND

BOTH a bloody civil war and an intense social revolution nearly ripped Mexico apart until Venustiano Carranza succeeded in seizing power as Mexico's first successful revolutionary president. Carranza succeeded because his socioeconomic reforms attracted strong support from all except the foreign interests and a determined Mexican upper class. This support explains Carranza's ability to stay in power during the most turbulent years in Mexico's generally stormy history. A statesman who used nationalism both to define his stubbornly independent foreign policy and to unite the country's social classes, Carranza was a leader who initiated significant changes at home and abroad. When he attempted to impose a handpicked successor, however, Carranza violated a fundamental precept of the Mexican Revolution, namely, the development of a populist political process.

Carranza's place in history has never been well defined. Until very recently, most historians considered Carranza at best a political moderate and often little more than a conservative hangover from the Porfirian dictatorship that preceded the Mexican Revolution in 1910. This attitude is partly explained by the fact that Carranza's archive of over twenty thousand documents was not available to researchers until 1969.[1] In any case, historians tend to emphasize the role of Pancho Villa, Emiliano Zapata, or Francisco Madero, even though Carranza was the real winner during the years of struggle, 1910 to 1920.[2] More importantly, the reasons why Carranza was able to defeat his rivals and establish a fairly durable government are largely a mystery to historians. For one thing, the unprecedented level of violent conflict that gripped the country from 1913 to 1916 gave way to the relatively peaceful years that Mexico enjoyed from 1917 to 1920.

The significance of the Carranza years is extremely important. It was under Carranza that the nationalist goals of the Mexican Revolution were embodied in the new Constitution of 1917. These were also the years that witnessed the growth of the working-class movement and the first attempt by any Mexican government to establish land reform on an institutionalized basis. Moreover, Carranza's economic policies ran counter to established foreign economic interests and became one of the principal themes of Mexican nationalism that still endures today. Those policies jolted the social structure with a group of new individuals replacing those who had opposed Carranza,[3] a new group that backed him in return for employment and economic opportunity.[4] Despite the complexity of the socioeconomic factors that enabled him to crush his rivals, Carranza was also a leader as traditional as the fabled "man on horseback" in the political history of Latin America.

Carranza possessed outstanding qualities of leadership that enabled him to respond to social demands with skill and precision. As a leader, he was as comfortable with lowly aides tending to his campfire as he was with the country's serious new reformers. Despite being over fifty years of age when he formed his movement, Carranza was an energetic man who seemed never to sleep.

Carranza, the son of a prosperous Coahuilan rancher, was descended from Spanish Basque immigrants. He received a good education and was particularly fond of history. Tall, able to harangue listeners with a good speech when the occasion demanded, Carranza radiated a resolve—stubborn and determined might be a better way of describing him—that was much appreciated at a time in Mexican history when chaos seemed the order of the day.

After terminating his medical studies because of problems with his eyesight, Carranza worked for a time on his father's ranch. In Cuatro Ciénegas, Coahuila, he entered politics as head of the municipal government where he won recognition as an efficient administrator and a political independent. Encouraged by local popularity and angered by harassment from the governor, Carranza and his two brothers led a successful revolt in 1893 against the state government. Carranza thereafter became a senator in the national legislature and began plotting the end of the Díaz dictatorship, which had ruled Mexico since 1876. It is important to remember that Carranza was never peacefully coopted into the Díaz system; he had to shoot his way in. With the fall of Díaz in 1911, Carranza became governor of Coahuila and served from May 1911 to March 1913.

As governor of Coahuila, Carranza pursued reform with a zeal that won the loyalties of the overwhelming majority of the state's inhabitants. The social programs he introduced included tough regulation of state concessionaires, progressive taxation, improved working conditions, support of strikes, recognition of unions, and dramatic educational reforms.[5]

One might reasonably argue that the Mexican Revolution really began in earnest when Carranza assumed leadership of the forces that opposed the dictatorship of Victoriano Huerta, the last antirevolutionary government. Despite conflicting interpretations of Carranza's place in Mexican history, there are few who would disagree with the proposition that Carranza's leadership was essential in enabling the revolutionaries to triumph. Carranza, the first leader to contest the political legitimacy of a government born out of assassination, issued a call in February 1913 for others to join him in toppling the Huerta government. Almost immediately, Carranza received enthusiastic support from Coahuilans willing to preserve their reforms by siding with their governor who now headed a national revolution.

Who joined this revolutionary movement that was initially labeled "constitutionalist"? The answer is that the supporters were from virtually every social class. There were urban petty bourgeoisie and small landowners from the interior who wanted jobs, credit, economic growth along nationalist lines, and political reform. Many were political radicals who called for an end to capitalism and demanded a thoroughgoing social revolution. Carranza's response was cautious and pragmatic. First, he hammered out a political manifesto that he hoped would attract the support of other political leaders.

Venustiano Carranza signing his first law as constitutional president of Mexico in May 1917

Constitutionalist encampment at Ramos Arizpe, Coahuila, in March 1913

Headquarters and fortifications of the early Constitutionalist movement in the Sierra Mojada of northeastern Mexico, March 1913

Mounted rebel troops assembling outside Monclova in March 1913

Revolutionary soldier opening fire from trench

Forces of Gen. Pablo González in Monclova, March 1913

Constitutionalist soldier defending railroad car, 1913

Burial of soldiers killed during the fighting for Tepexpán, state of México, in June 1915

Soldadera in formation with other rebel troops, 1913

Villagers of Cadereyta, Nuevo León, welcoming *carrancista* forces in October 1915

Clothes being distributed to poor children in Mexico City

Indian contingent preparing to enter Cinco de Mayo parade in 1916

Slogans and crowd meet government train in Monterrey

Arrival of U.S. authorities across the International Bridge in Nuevo Laredo

Public gathering at the Palacio Municipal of Matamoros in December 1915

Motor convoy crossing the mountains of Nuevo León

Political rally being carried out at the railroad station of San Pedro de las Colonias, Coahuila

Railroad workers in 1920

Venustiano Carranza reviews his troops in Veracruz

Alvaro Obregón posing with Yaqui soldiers from Sonora

The Monument to the Revolution, Mexico City, where the remains of Villa, Madero, Carranza, Calles, and Cardenas are deposited

All photographs in this section courtesy of Centro de Estudios de Historia de México

The political document that temporarily united his supporters was the Plan de Guadalupe, named after the hacienda where it was signed. The Plan de Guadalupe was not a call for social revolution but merely a statement of general goals for toppling the Huerta dictatorship. The document declared that Huerta was no longer the chief executive of the country and that all his acts were repudiated. Until new elections could be held, people were given thirty days in which to recognize Carranza as interim executive. Anyone not recognizing him during that period was to be considered an enemy.

Carranza initially told his followers that social and economic reforms would have to wait until a newly elected national legislature ratified them. Carranza, however, began issuing decrees almost immediately in response to popular grievances, decrees that had the force of law and were later incorporated into the national constitution. By the summer of 1913, Carranza himself began calling for recognition of the class struggle.

The united front led by Carranza presented a strong and unified northern opposition to Huerta. Although other regional leaders attacked Huerta, the Constitutionalist movement under Carranza was his major challenge.

The first to join Carranza were leaders in Chihuahua and Sonora. Both of these states had benefited from progressive governors during the generally conservative Madero government that had preceded Huerta. In Sonora, however, military firebrands such as Alvaro Obregón, Benjamín Hill, Plutarco Elías Calles, Salvador Alvarado, and Manuel Diéguez seized control of the government. They did so when the *maderista* governor, José María Maytorena, limped across the state line to Arizona, having lost his stomach for the fight. These pro-Carranza petty bourgeoisie demanded the reforms that reflected the basic needs of the country's impoverished masses.[6]

In Chihuahua, the state's political destinies were largely in the hands of Francisco "Pancho" Villa. Villa gained the support of those who enjoyed the progressive reforms enacted by another Madero stalwart, Abraham González. After Huerta forces assassinated González, Villa stepped into the political vacuum as a charismatic guerrilla tactician who soon amassed a formidable army.

Together, these groups constituted a military force

forged out of the country's disaffected majority. They would eventually smash Mexico's weakened army, which had done little to distinguish itself for almost fifty years. Lined up outside their adobe huts in the summer of 1913, these forces were as confident as they were determined to crush a hated order that had forced most of them to live in the most abject poverty. The old federal army, by 1914, was no match for them. One of the most significant factors in Huerta's defeat was that few were willing to respond to his call to defend the regime. Men drafted into Huerta's army often broke and fled after being released from the chains that had held them in railroad cars.

The process by which the rebel forces allied themselves with Carranza accelerated the national character of the movement. Carranza ordered all local *jefes* to submit to his authority or be considered opponents. Most were willing to submit because Carranza's movement had been highly organized from the beginning. Carranza maintained strong control over military matters as well as the emerging government. Although he preferred administration, Carranza personally led cavalry charges in the early days before confining himself to political leadership. Those forces loyal to Carranza had only to enforce his decrees in their areas of jurisdiction. In return they received arms and ammunition as well as detailed political instructions.

The success of Carranza's reforms attracted increasing numbers of recruits. The army grew and embarked upon a spring offensive in 1914 that gradually advanced to Mexico City in August. Huerta fled the country and Carranza seemed to be in charge of the nation's destinies on the eve of civil war. This time Carranza found himself pitted against the forces of Pancho Villa and Emiliano Zapata.

One of the great mysteries of the Mexican Revolution was how the two leaders—Villa and Zapata—who presumably represented the ideals of the Revolution were so convincingly defeated by Carranza within such a relatively short time. From the resumption of strife in November 1914 until the fall of 1915, the adversaries slashed away at one another until Carranza was able to assert control.

The turning point arrived in the spring of 1915. After

two crushing defeats inflicted on Villa at Celaya in April, Carranza dominated the situation. By reading captured documents, the *carrancistas* learned that the *villistas* could not even obtain seven-millimeter ammunition in May.[7] That same month, Pablo González, one of Carranza's generals, occupied Saltillo and declared that the northern border was effectively in the hands of Carranza's forces. Confident that Villa was finished, González suggested a southern advance.[8] Although Villa did try to send arms to Zapata in July 1915, Carranza's generals frustrated this attempt, thus symbolizing the inability of Villa and Zapata to carry out joint campaigns.[9] Isolated from each other, Villa and Zapata hung on as guerrilla leaders in Chihuahua and Morelos, annoyances rather than a major preoccupation for Carranza's government.

Carranza triumphed over Villa and Zapata because he broadened the base of his political support. Early political pamphlets indicate that Carranza pictured himself as a social revolutionary much earlier than is commonly recognized. His attempt at a pluralistic class union on the basis of nationalism meant an effort to serve the needs of all but the intransigent upper classes, at least in rhetorical terms. The strictly political items were the reestablishment of local judicial and legislative powers in each of the states. Respect for self-government was a precept that the *carrancistas* piously promised.[10] A continuously frustrated middle class that had only begun to enjoy such rights in the days of Madero therefore supported Carranza enthusiastically. The petty bourgeoisie also wanted to retain their positions in Carranza's army, bureaucracy, and newspapers, as well as in teaching positions.

For the masses in general, Carranza's reforms were generally far more comprehensive than those of Zapata and Villa. Of all the early leaders, Carranza adopted the toughest policy against the Church, even though the rank-and-file of his followers seemed to call for a more militant policy. Carranza's policy of exiling priests, seizing Church property, and confiscating Church wealth gradually moderated as Carranza smashed the clerical supporters more quickly than anybody had anticipated.

A particularly popular policy adopted by the *carrancistas* was feeding the hungry by bringing in foodstuffs to particularly hard-hit areas. With the economy severely disrupted, many areas had been on the verge of starvation for several years. Carranza forced merchants to sell their goods at low prices. Since merchants were usually foreigners, such as Chinese and Spaniards, they were particularly hated. Carranza made the most of this bitterness by hitting the merchants hard when they attempted to raise their prices.

As Carranza surveyed the scope of his movement, he could certainly reflect that social reforms had a direct bearing upon his political success. This relation was also true with regard to his land policies. Those who opposed him simply had their lands seized for being "enemies of the people." These lands were then usually turned over to agents acting on behalf of a special government program designed to see to it that political enemies could not use their wealth to foment opposition to the Carranza government.

The land was generally not taken for the purpose of distributing it to the landless poor; instead, it was administered by loyal followers who tended to maintain their grip on such properties. For the masses, Carranza offered provisional title to communal properties taken from them earlier by the Porfirian dictatorship. Carranza's basic policy was that of returning the lands seized from the peasants since the 1850s. He also decreed that villages and municipalities in the rural areas should receive some lands expropriated from the big landowners. Many villagers also received lands from sympathetic army officers, followed by definitive land titles issued by Carranza. The amount of land taken through unofficial means by the *carrancistas* from the traditional hacienda class has never been calculated, but it was undoubtedly a great deal.

For labor, Carranza appeared as the early champion of the working-class movement. Carranza always called for better working conditions, the formation of unions, and periodic pay raises. The decrees that ended the company stores and peonage were important factors in Carranza's popularity. Moreover, Carranza personally intervened in many strikes to see that the workers received what they wanted.

More often than not, the *carrancistas* were received with enthusiasm when they began extending their social reforms over the nation. For many, such changes represented the hope that schools would be established, since Carranza called for a vastly expanded educational network. Another feature of Carranza's program was his concern for better governmental services. Many of Carranza's local leaders embarked upon ambitious public works programs to build roads, public buildings, and parks. They also instituted progressive taxation policies that forced owners either to put their land into production or to offer it for sale. The added tax revenues meant more jobs and local improvements. Moreover, many local laws, often dictated by Carranza, forced owners of apartments to comply with rent freezes and time limits when tenants could be evicted.

The new political leadership reflected the country's roots more than at any other time in Mexican history. At a time of conflict and unprecedented confusion, the *carrancistas* knew that a loss of their mass political support spelled certain defeat. That no other faction was able to contest their role after 1915 attests to their skill in identifying problems and implementing solutions. A major reason for the weakness of the opposition to Carranza in such key states as Puebla, Veracruz, Yucatán, Sonora, Coahuila, and San Luis Potosí is that the *carrancista* political leadership in these areas was simply too effective in dealing with local issues.

While *carrancistas* accelerated and expanded the scope of their victory, there were those who doubted. Was the Carranza victory a genuine social revolution? For any revolution to be successful it must overturn the dominant forces that control the forces of production. In this respect, Carranza reshuffled the composition of Mexico's class system and banished many from high status and privileges. These issues were so hotly contested that at least one million people died out of a population of only fifteen million. Hundreds of thousands more fled the country permanently, thus beginning the first significant wave of Mexican immigration to the United States.

The battles won by Carranza meant that institutions such as the army, the unions, and the bureaucracy would be oriented toward a program of national unity rather than the narrow interests of the Church, foreign investors, and hacienda owners. Urban and rural workers experienced a definite change in social status and economic gain in terms of wages and public services. The governments of Mexico would no longer be composed of whites oriented to Europe and openly despising the native masses as had been true throughout the nineteenth century. A significant feature of Carranza's movement was the determination to encourage pride in the nation's customs and Indian roots, a sharp break with the policies of past Mexican governments.

The military victory alone reflected major changes. Women serving as soldiers was one example. According to many sources, most of the famous *soldaderas* were *carrancistas*. With a pistol in her belt, rifle in hand, and cartridges slung across her chest, the *soldadera* was as rugged as any male soldier. Chroniclers of the Mexican Revolution recall that *soldaderas* were often seen picking up the rifles of fallen comrades and charging ahead.

What made women fight for Carranza? For one thing, Carranza encouraged feminist groups to organize, and he subsidized their magazines and speaking tours. Moreover, he decreed divorce laws and generally encouraged the independent development of women in a country often dripping with machismo. This was a somewhat risky political venture that might have backfired on Carranza, but it was also a legitimate social demand. Women thereafter were able to establish careers in heretofore forbidden areas and to take more conspicuous parts as nurses, teachers, and officials in the regime when it increased its attention to social reforms.

The new army thus had an emotional stake in the durability of the Carranza government. The nationalistic transformation of the political culture in Mexico resulted in part from the fact that thousands of soldiers journeyed far from the remote areas that they had grown up in and began to identify with the rest of Mexico. In the process, the army became the one national institution in the country and one of the strongest defenders of national reforms. Although many perished, their fellow soldiers were proud of the task that they had accomplished and believed that a new Mexico was being constructed.

The generals who directed this army of peons, railroad workers, cowboys, miners, and drifters have probably not received the credit they deserve. Carranza's army, after early 1915, was rarely defeated in the field. These improvised military leaders who began as novices in 1913 were successful in maintaining political order by repeatedly crushing the almost daily challenges to Carranza's rule.

Seldom flashy and usually sober types who avoided the limelight, Carranza's generals were normally glad to leave military duty. All of them respected Carranza, for the First Chief often dictated strategy himself and made sure that they received sufficient supplies and arms. Their real power, however, was based on their popularity in the many areas where the army had shown early concern for reforms. The generals knew that any slackening in their political idealism would result in a corresponding drop in recruits. Thus the generals were among the most enthusiastic supporters of revolutionary goals, at least until 1917.

Even as Carranza toured villages after the defeat of Villa and Zapata, he was aware that serious tasks lay ahead. The most crucial question he had to answer was how to reconstruct the country and resolve its economic problems. Large sections of the nation were devastated after the war. The railroads barely functioned because fuel, experienced hands, rolling stock, and operating rail lines were in short supply. Mexico had to develop its exports in order to purchase needed industrial products. The country also lacked investment capital because traditionally conservative investors had sought landholding as the best means of financial security.

Asking his followers to support a policy of economic nationalism, Carranza was successful in revitalizing Mexico's economy. His policy called for increased regulation of the economy by the government so that redistribution of Mexico's wealth would benefit general economic development, especially the well-being of lower and middle classes. The first steps were the seizure of the railroads and federalization of the rivers so that water disputes would be settled by the central government.

The financial steps in Carranza's new reform program were perhaps the most carefully thought out. Carranza avoided the political problems of foreign loans when he simply printed his own currency. The government also repudiated several questionable foreign loans contracted by past regimes, thus emerging with few international obligations.

Carranza hit banks particularly hard. Previously, they had issued banknotes out of proportion to their reserves and had extended credit liberally to personal favorites. Carranza forced many banks to close when they could not comply with his decrees that obliged them to maintain an equal amount of bullion reserves in proportion to circulating bank notes. Prosperous banks that refused were physically occupied and directed by government administrators. Carranza attempted to establish a single bank of emissions in order to rationalize currency emissions. Such a bank had been one of his most frequent promises, a pledge he was unable to redeem. One of his most popular decrees stated that all past debts owed by individuals were invalid.

One of the country's most consistent and emotional demands was for a better arrangement with the foreign economic interests that traditionally exploited Mexico's natural wealth. Carranza took over the two largest banks, both of which were foreign owned. He also began strict regulation of mines and oil concessions; previous governments had given such concessions to foreigners with few advantages for Mexico. Carranza increased tax rates and forced foreign investors to comply with government regulations concerning drilling rights, leasing arrangements, and labor disputes.

At one point, Carranza ordered all mines to renew operations or face expropriation. Such a demand was unprecedented in 1916; but with the masses it was extremely popular as part of a drive to force outsiders to respect Mexican law. By carefully regulating the growth of foreign investments, Carranza attempted to encourage the development of Mexican entrepreneurs who would replace the foreigners and place the economic destinies of Mexico in the hands of its nationals.[11]

Both Carranza and his governors encouraged Mexican miners and oil producers as much as possible. Such encouragement usually meant favored government purchasing policies, sliding tax rates designed to aid smaller Mexican firms, and tariff concessions.[12] Carranza himself often decided which mine owners and industrialists could receive scarce supplies of coal and oil and have priority for rail transport.

The government's early financial problems made difficult decisions inevitable. Although Carranza's decision to print his own money enabled him to pursue independent policies, Mexico suffered from serious currency depreciation until December 1916. The government tried to respond to the needs of various companies by sending new batches of paper money to areas where currency was lacking. In other cases, the government authorized mines to remit small coins that the miners themselves produced.[13] Nevertheless, inflation was so bad that soldiers complained that they could not afford to buy cigarettes, while merchants often refused to accept paper money.[14] Finally, bowing to the demands of local authorities and the population in general, the government returned to metal currency by January 1917. Inflation was not a problem thereafter; in fact, Mexico enjoyed financial stability for the next four years.

Although Carranza could enjoy the luxury of a country dinner on local haciendas, the land question remained a critical issue that affected the outlines of political economy and rural support for the newly established regime. The key fact is that from 1914 to 1917 agricultural production declined, sometimes precipitously, in practically every state. If inflation was the most pressing early difficulty facing the government, the other serious problem was the lack of foodstuffs. Frosts and plagues of locusts further weakened agricultural production during the crucial years 1915 and 1916. The government found itself in an unpleasant bind, what with civil war, foreign intervention, starvation, and land-hungry *campesinos* demanding land for their own use.

Another reason for food shortages was that the earlier Porfirian policies had favored the production of such luxury goods as coffee, sugar, and tobacco for export rather than the production of common foodstuffs. Carranza responded by revising tariff policies to prohibit the export of corn, beans, cattle, and most other food items to try to force merchants to sell these goods on the national market. Customs officials and army units received strict orders to apprehend smugglers. Shutting off the export trade was one solution to the food shortage problem.

How was Carranza to increase food production? The situation was so critical that Carranza ordered that captured hides and cattle taken from the *villistas* be exchanged across the border for corn and other badly needed items.[15] Another remedy that the government attempted was a mechanization of the agricultural sector. Carranza helped formulate the policies that brought tractors to Mexico for the first time. Railroad platforms hauled crude prototypes of these modern machines to isolated parts of rural Mexico. Government engineers then demonstrated their use to farmers in the hope that enough of them would be purchased to stimulate production.

Since the *carrancista* forces attracted great numbers of *campesinos* because of their repeated promises to distribute land, Carranza was committed to some kind of land reform. As the regime wore on, land seized during the Porfiriato was returned and *ejido* lands distributed. In all, about 200,000 hectares went to the *campesinos*. After 1916, however, Carranza also began returning lands seized from prominent *hacendados* taken during the period from 1913 to 1915. This was done to increase food production and ensure political support in the countryside. Carranza always maintained that lasting agrarian reform could not really be accomplished until the government could provide increased, large-scale credit and technical assistance. Until then, he maintained, further division of land would only accelerate the decline in food production. This dilemma has continued in agrarian reform in Mexico today—social justice or hunger.

As in the case of land reform, Carranza also had to satisfy the growing working-class movement that was such a vital factor in his rise to power. His alliance with the working class began when he met with the leaders of the Casa del Obrero Mundial in August 1914. This anarchosyndicalist organization initiated the first clearly defined working-class struggles during the Madero years. Gradually the leadership responded favorably to Carranza's early support of workers throughout the country. The radical leaders received Carranza's permission to organize unions and strike for higher pay so long as they did not question either his governmental policies or his leadership of the Revolution. The government therefore intervened in strikes both to squelch radical agitators who could accelerate the radicalization of the labor movement and to guarantee that the economy kept functioning.

The fact that Carranza would favor militant workers up to a certain limit points out one of the contradictions in trying to establish a nationalist, multiclass ideology. Carranza did not want to alienate his budding support among the new bourgeois entrepreneurial class that he was trying to build.

So, in February 1916, Carranza ordered that Casa officials stop radicalizing working-class politics. When the Casa del Obrero Mundial called for a general strike in August 1916, Carranza broke with the radical labor leaders for good.

Crushing the strike strained, but did not weaken, Carranza's general worker support. The anarchosyndicalists called for the general strike because they were dissatisfied with the slow progress in resolving the currency crisis. The strikers received little support from the general public; consequently Carranza was able to crush the strike quickly. The radicals of the Casa del Obrero Mundial were not a force to be reckoned with thereafter.

Instead, the urban working class seems to have been fairly contented with Carranza's peace and the economic revival after December 1916. Railroad workers, for example, received good pay and benefits that included educational programs and pensions as part of the new government policy of railroad regulation. If Carranza had lost his taste for strong support of a radical working-class movement, he certainly did not abandon the labor movement. Out of gratitude, labor did not support any of the several ill-fated attempts to topple Carranza until 1920.

Workers played a key part in Carranza's 1917 presidential election. Workers campaigned for him because Carranza continued to exert pressure on employers to pay fair wages, and he went to extra lengths to see that those hurt by unemployment received funds directly from the federal treasury.[16] Carranza received hundreds of telegrams from local unions allied with local political parties reiterating their support for past favors. In some cases, these commitments also involved unions that organized rural as well as urban workers.[17] Carranza also gave the unions the freedom to forge their own national union, the Confederación Regional Obrera Mexicana (CROM), when they met in 1918 to solidify their pact. Although Carranza wanted leadership more to his liking, the new national labor union was able to maintain its independence without the heavy-handed interference characteristic of later Mexican governments.

The social structure that Carranza inherited was seriously underdeveloped. Nearly 80 percent of Mexico's five million economically active inhabitants worked in the agricultural sector. Commerce and finance employed a petty bourgeoisie of a mere 5 percent. The rest engaged in mining, industry, and the service sector. The social structure was also weakened by high rates of infant mortality, alcoholism, and traditional illnesses, such as typhus, stomach disorders, and influenza.

Carranza hoped that education would overcome at least some of the social problems; but education yielded promising but eventually disappointing results. Carranza dramatized his faith in education by personally placing the first stones in ceremonies dedicating new schools for teachers. These were events of no small importance since the people desperately yearned for a better way of life. Such acts also cemented the ties between local inhabitants and their governors who proudly inaugurated libraries as well as schools.[18]

The major problem was Carranza's belief that municipal government should control local educational policy. Carranza hoped that citizens and rulers would profit by casting off the old and tightly centralized policies of the past. The success that locally controlled education enjoyed in Carranza's native Coahuila, however, was not always repeated in the rest of the country.[19]

All the same, Carranza could claim that significant achievements also took place. For the first time, people had access to newly established schools for the blind, deaf-mutes, and the mentally retarded. The medical school received ample funding, as did a string of newly established industrial and technical schools. New statutes provided school children with medical clinics, better administration, and textbooks, which presented the country's history in highly nationalistic terms. Pupils were thus indoctrinated with such potent ideas as racial unity, the superiority of contributions made by the mestizo majority, and an appreciation for Mexico's Indian heritage.

The needy and destitute were another concern of the Carranza government. Conscientious representatives of the government, such as Gen. López de Lara in Mexico City, often appeared in public to give clothing to poor children. The government also established public dormitories, schools for orphans, and child-care centers for working mothers. Other social policies involved progressive tax laws, rent ordinances that gave greater security to marginal tenants, and a practice of attending to personal requests for jobs and audiences with Carranza.

The Carranza epoch was notable for its legislative attempts to cleanse the social order. Many local governments outlawed prostitution and the sale of intoxicating beverages, in some cases under the threat of the death penalty. Carranza outlawed bullfights, cockfights, and gambling and restricted the activities of pawnshops. Mexico City once again emerged as a beautiful city with clean parks, good public transportation, and improved health inspectors.

The government's aggressive foreign policy encouraged a collective unity with the new regime. Carranza revived the memory of the Niños Héroes in tribute to the six cadets who died defending Chapultepec Castle when it was overrun by United States forces in September 1847. Diplomatic and military confrontations between Carranza and Woodrow Wilson emphasized Carranza's determination to win respect for Mexico both at home and abroad.

Popular support for the government reached its zenith during such tense episodes as the Pershing Expedition from the United States into Mexico. Thousands of citizens from every social class asked for arms and military training in order to turn back the North American forces. Patriotism was often linked to the defense of social reforms and the nation itself. Another manifestation of the growing sense of nationhood that Carranza encouraged was manifested in locally organized fiestas to help flood victims. This collaborative attitude even affected a few *hacendados* who, in some instances, provided land for those in need.[20]

The success that popular reforms enjoyed during Carranza's years in power meant that he could pose as an authoritarian populist. Few could hope to overturn the alliance between politics and society since the army and Carranza's social policies added security and self-respect to his cause. Close supervision of politics in the interior enabled Carranza to consolidate his power. Furthermore, the 1917 Constitution embodied the ideal of an aroused society and is still the law of the land as well as an expression of the hopes and dreams of the Mexican Revolution.

Carranza opened the constituent assembly to all his supporters during what many consider some of the fairest elections ever held in Mexico. The elections produced a group of politically inexperienced, but talented, young legislators who gathered at Querétaro to write what at the time was the most progressive national charter in the world. Those elected were all *carrancistas*, but gradually they divided into conservative and radical factions.

The radicals assumed control of the convention and dictated the constitution that Carranza finally promised to obey. In great detail, the 1917 Constitution defined labor legislation, Church restrictions, reforms in education, and the nation's inalienable ownership of its subsoil wealth. Initially troubled that these measures were placed in the constitution instead of being legislated as general laws, Carranza sat in the chambers and did not intervene in the hot floor disputes. Carranza was surprised that the radicals overturned his milder proposals but soon became a strong defender of the new constitution except for the most extreme Church restrictions. The agreement upon the reforms that had cost so much blood in the past was a big factor in the general peace that Mexico gradually enjoyed after 1917.[21]

With a strong mandate to rule and backed up by a constitution that made social reform the law, Carranza could easily pose as a champion of the previously scorned masses. The Constitution of 1917 was therefore a powerful weapon against domestic conservatives and external economic interests. The national government had great power and the army was strong enough to crush anybody who disputed the new order. The Church, the country's other major establishment, lost much of its power because it had supported the wrong side during the Revolution. Therefore, the Church could do little when the government began encouraging the spread of secular education, providing social services on a greater scale, and trying to place ideology and patriotism above Catholicism.

Carranza's style of government involved a careful balancing of interests while ensuring that his authority was the ultimate arbitrator of all affairs. As adept at receiving a wreath of flowers as in disciplining an unruly governor, Carranza was the precursor of the strong executives who have characterized twentieth-century Mexico.

Carranza was authoritarian, but he interpreted this

stance as a form of populism in which the support of the majority was his mandate to decide and to execute national policy. For Carranza and the nationalists who supported him, a strong executive was the only agency for swift government action. At a time when the national legislature and parliamentary niceties had lost the admiration they had enjoyed in the midnineteenth century and the political parties were still struggling to present themselves as contenders for power, Carranza became the surrogate for those who had taken over through armed struggle during the bloody days of the Revolution. He may appropriately be called a populist because he rejected the liberal ideas that had failed to bring the country success and because he ignored the hairsplitting that put legislative technique above social justice.[22]

Carranza was certainly not the classical dictator who had often presided over the destinies of Mexico. He was accessible for an easygoing chat with the most downtrodden of his supporters. Never a leader who was feared more than he was respected, his own austerity and devotion to work gave him more the air of a modern Philip II of Spain. Carranza presented an appealing sight to many as he performed his daily gallop from Chapultepec Castle to the office of the national executive at the Zócalo. Carranza may have been a patrician figure, but he was too far removed from the old order ever to consider a return to the empty clichés, easy compromises, and unrealistic goals of the past.

Mexico's new president was certainly a cut above the average citizen, but this did not prevent his strolling through Mexico City's Merced Market like any ordinary shopper. Citizens looked at him with respect because Carranza exuded a tough idealism in defining and pursuing the goals of national reconstruction. Although he lacked the charismatic qualities of some other leaders, Carranza's personal quest for greatness was nonetheless a mixture of humility and grandeur, traits somewhat difficult to reconcile but, all the same, unmistakable parts of the Mexican Revolution. In retrospect, it is now clear that Carranza symbolized that transition between the gaslight era and the powerful social revolution that was beginning at this time in the non-Western world.

As he rode in the ceremonial carriage to be sworn in as president in 1917, Carranza was at the height of his power.

The government that Carranza established was a well-run machine that reasserted the central government's control over affairs in the interior. Factors in his success were boundless energy, careful attention to administrative detail, and organization. Carranza's government prided itself on its neat efficiency and behind-the-scenes politicking. Carranza insisted on having the final word in even the smallest affair of government. By means of retaining firm patriarchal control of the bureaucracy and maintaining a steady political correspondence with his subordinates, Carranza was determined to rule as a strong executive.

The chief executive and his cabinet wielded real power and took advantage of every opportunity to entrench themselves. The ministers and officials who surrounded Carranza were usually young and dynamic reformers. The president took pains to maintain friendly alliances with favored newspapers and made use of such propaganda outlets as the Commission of Constitutionalist Propaganda and Study. The head of this agency dutifully promised to "make publicly known your policy of intense nationalism" in October 1916.[23] The relatively slow development of political parties and the uninspired performance of the national legislature enabled Carranza to press his claim that he voiced the national will.

Carranza also had a unique relation with the governors of the various Mexican states. It was a fact of political life that by late 1916 they were checking with Carranza before carrying out not only every important proposal but petty matters as well. They had to ask the executive when to authorize new elections for the municipalities,[24] and they competed for state military units even as Carranza himself had once done. Carranza, however, had little faith in the political reliability of the governors and decided that it was unwise for them to have both political and military jurisdiction simultaneously. For fear of political strife, Carranza decided early that no governor should ever have more than fifteen hundred troops at his disposal.[25]

Despite their subordinate role to the chief executive, many governors played a significant role in solidifying the regime. In general, states ravaged by warfare and insurrections were usually those in which local reforms were at a premium. Those governors who lost their nerve during difficult times—usually from some local military challenge—were replaced with veterans trusted by Carranza. Carranza's intervention into local matters was invariably beneficial. Local politics tended to be rough; and many governors were quick to jail, beat, or otherwise close down any opposition, despite Carranza's frequent efforts to restrain them. Cut from a different slice of the social order from Carranza's, these political figures were often inexperienced and politically clumsy. It should be said in their defense that they managed to maintain relative peace until 1920, which was no mean feat and something that Mexico desperately wanted.

Guanajuato was one example of how effective local government operated in the interior. This state experienced relatively little armed opposition because of the abilities of the first *carrancista* governor, Gen. José Siurob. At one point, Carranza gave Siurob permission to campaign in all of the districts of the state, a typical desire of the most rabid *carrancista* governors. In this case, Siurob felt that peace in Guanajuato depended upon making sure that Carranza's reforms were enforced. The reforms that interested Governor Siurob the most were school construction, the division and redistribution of sixteen haciendas owned by the clergy, food dispensations to the poor, and increased salaries, as well as pensions, for workers.

Guanajuato ran out of food during a general crisis that both federal and state authorities responded to by acting quickly. The food shortage was accentuated by slow-moving trains trying to leave the congested railheads. Higher taxes and wage increases decreed by Governor Siurob for the miners also slowed economic growth. The mine owners responded by closing down the mines and throwing miners out of work. To help correct the problem, Carranza provided free rail service for workers in Guanajuato so that they could find jobs in other areas. He also sent 10,000 pesos to the Guanajuato relief agency specifically organized to provide relief for the miners.[26] Finally, Carranza forced foreign mine owners to reopen, even though they were still reluctant to obey the new legislation.

Guanajuato was also a good example of a state that benefited from accelerated outlays for social services, including inoculation programs and hospitals. The governor's construction campaign tripled the number of schools. Siurob continued to journey into the countryside holding conferences on the ideals and goals that the *carrancistas* wanted to implement. Siurob's real purpose in these journeys was to line up cooperative candidates for reformist economic policies and improved municipal services. Replaced in December 1916 for not being able to wipe out troublesome bandits plaguing the state, Siurob left in his place a hard-nosed general.[27] He had kept the state loyal to Carranza and departed on the eve of the orderly years of the First Chief's presidency.

The most consistently nationalistic feature of Carranza's government was his foreign policy. A mixture of stubborn pride and desire for national development was the formula that made him successful. In addition, Carranza carefully expanded Mexican diplomacy into the world arena by taking advantage of the unsettled situation that developed during World War I. Repeatedly the victim of past aggressions, and eager for economic independence, Mexican society steadfastly backed Carranza's unrelenting defense of national sovereignty.

Carranza's relations with the United States were stormy, with one crisis after another. Carranza soon discovered that President Woodrow Wilson was determined to maintain the economic interests of the United States in nearly every phase of his dealings with Mexico. Carranza protested the North American occupation of Veracruz and was the only leader of the Revolution that did. Even when it was apparent that Carranza had defeated Huerta, the attempts by Wilson to arbitrate the situation so that someone other than Carranza would rule Mexico infuriated the First Chief. Carranza warned the ABC ministers (of Argentina, Brazil, and Chile) that the civil war in Mexico was independent of their mediation and that he would not suspend hostilities, proudly adding that he led "a people in arms" and "represented the interests of my fatherland."[28]

Huerta, because he was losing the conflict, grasped at the ABC armistice proposal by stating it was "very probable" that he and the *carrancistas* could arrive at an understanding for "the complete pacification of the country."[29] Carranza expressed doubts that the views of the ABC ministers represented the official attitudes of their governments.[30]

Negotiations for de facto recognition of Carranza by the United States dragged on for months. The United States demanded that Carranza protect North American investments and that he pledge to stop harassment of the Church, to end property seizures, and to make war damage payments. Carranza refused, saying that policy concerning such matters would be determined later by new legislation. Carranza's philosophy—the Carranza Doctrine, as it was later called—demanded respect between all nations as well as an end to foreign intervention in domestic affairs. Mexican officials were quick to point out that the United States did not want mediation in its own internal affairs during its Civil War. Carranza's consistent position was that intervention and foreign mediation in Mexico were unjustified and would not be tolerated.[31] Forced to admit that Carranza controlled Mexico and nervous about the European war, Wilson finally granted Carranza de facto recognition in October 1915.

The northern border with the United States was the locale for a number of Carranza's diplomatic confrontations. Carranza was particularly outraged at the poor treatment suffered by Mexican immigrants in the United States. Clashes between northern Mexican villagers and United States troops had occurred intermittently for years. As early as April 1914, Carranza ordered all his consulates to report hostile movements to him, as well as any other matter that it would be "convenient to know."[32] Mexican secret service agents watched carefully the activities of counterrevolutionary groups hostile to Carranza that were located in the United States Southwest and reported that they had links with some big North American investors. Carranza also established several newspapers along the border and consistently stressed the need for decent working conditions for Mexican migrant workers in the United States.

Probably Carranza's most daring move was his support of a Mexican-American revolt in south Texas which began in 1915 and continued intermittently until late 1916. Except for the black revolts in the 1960s, this conflict was the most serious uprising by any North American ethnic group in the twentieth century and hundreds undoubtedly lost their lives. Carranza, backing the rebels with regular army troops sent over the Río Grande into Texas, drew up plans for the Mexican Army to seize strategic zones along the border with a view to linking up with Mexican insurgents in Texas. Since Carranza had chosen the leaders of the revolt and furnished them aid, he could determine the outcome. When the revolt fizzled out, Carranza sacked its leaders and confined himself to other endeavors in order to stave off North American intervention in Mexico.

The most notable event that took place along the northern border was the Pershing Expedition, launched shortly after Pancho Villa's attack on Columbus, New Mexico, on March 9, 1916. The arrival of North American troops on Mexican soil to apprehend Villa caught Carranza by surprise. He finally ordered that Pershing's forces advance no further. Fighting broke out when Carranza ordered his generals to engage United States forces if they advanced, a decision which resulted in a Mexican victory at Carrizal. Carranza resisted with confidence because Mexican society stood solidly behind its leader, demanding arms and quick action against the invaders. This stance represented a fundamental change in the attitude of northerners since they had not rallied against the North American troops during the Mexican War of 1847.

Conferences in Atlantic City, New Jersey, to end the threat of all-out war centered on attempts to force Carranza to curtail his social and economic reforms. Carranza had decreed greatly increased taxes and oil, mining, and banking regulations, which the U.S. State Department absolutely opposed. Throughout these negotiations, Carranza firmly rejected demands to end his restrictions, insisting that internal Mexican affairs were not proper subjects for discussion. He did so even when the United States offered de jure diplomatic recognition as an inducement.[33]

Carranza finally won the deadlock when weary United States negotiators announced unilateral withdrawal from Mexico. Even after the controversy over the Pershing Expedition ended, Wilson continued to protest Carranza's increasingly strict regulation of Mexico's natural resources. Carranza eventually forced foreign investors, including those from the United States, to recognize Mexican law, even at the risk of war.

Mexican neutrality during World War I represented a defiance of the United States that appealed to national pride.

Carranza's courting of the Germans resulted in the famous Zimmerman Telegram, an offer by Germany involving the return of former Mexican territory lost to the United States after the Mexican War in return for a military alliance with the Kaiser. The whole affair, of course, was contingent upon a German victory in the war. This telegram was such a serious escalation of tensions that it was a decisive factor in Wilson's asking Congress to declare war upon Germany.

Carranza was tempted to join the Germans but knew that involving Mexico in war would have been ruinous. His silence on the matter only added to Wilson's fear concerning Mexican aims. This uncertainty was what Carranza wanted, because Mexico's using the Germans as a potential ally forced Wilson to hesitate before considering further intervention in Mexican affairs.

Another country of crucial importance to Mexico was Japan. Carranza needed arms and once the United States market was shut off to him, he placed several large orders for Japanese munitions. Japan aided Carranza considerably by selling him the machinery to establish a Mexican arms industry capable of turning out enough equipment to furnish the Mexican Army. The Zimmerman Telegram had also included a proposal whereby Mexico would try to influence Japan to change sides in the war with the promise of a free hand in the Far East in the event of a German victory.

Carranza's relations with Mexico's sister republics of Latin America consisted largely of pleas for stronger unity based on cultural and ethnic ties. Energetic Mexican diplomats insisted that Latin America join Mexico in opposing economic imperialism and Dollar Diplomacy intervention. Although there were usually no successful firm understandings in South America, Carranza did pursue a successful campaign in Central America that resulted in keeping hostile Guatemala from attacking the southern state of Chiapas along the Mexico-Guatemala border.

The ultimate success of Carranza's government depended upon the loyalty and performance of the army. Carranza supervised military affairs as closely as possible. Very early, Carranza ordered his Treasury officials never to release funds to army officers unless the release had his approval.[34] Since these were times when volunteers fought for a popular cause,

Carranza had to take special care that there was ideological purity in the officer corps. Unlike the *villistas* or *zapatistas*[35] *carrancistas* did not permit officers of the old federal army to join their ranks. Several times, Carranza ordered his generals to cashier reported conservatives or "reactionaries" in various military units.[36] The new president demanded that his officers not comment upon, or attempt to influence, diplomatic issues.

Even though he is usually remembered as a statesman, Carranza always made it clear that he was head of the army. Carranza asserted this role symbolically by taking part in target practice with his troops, but he also dictated strategy even to the point of controlling ammunition deliveries. Until the end, Carranza had the personal loyalty of most generals. Grizzled warriors like Gen. Manuel Diéguez were capable of writing Carranza fond letters stating that he stopped by Carranza's home in Coahuila to admire the olive trees that the chief executive had planted.[37] Yet those who disobeyed Carranza were arrested. One of the great changes that took place at this time was the replacement of the old professionals by young *carrancistas* who managed to grab land by one means or another. Some major industrialists of Mexico got their start in this way. Other *carrancistas* entered politics and remained there for generations.

In the course of carrying out the president's orders, the army distinguished itself by consistently defeating the government's opponents. The major participants in the early stages of the Mexican Revolution—Villa, Zapata, Huerta—were beaten after hard campaigns. After 1916, the army turned its attention to a variety of conservative opponents led by Félix Díaz, the nephew of the former dictator. Regional upstarts also had to be crushed in Veracruz, Chiapas, Oaxaca, and Michoacán. Bandits also took up much of the army's time and energy in nearly every state of the republic.

Since army officers were often governors or political candidates, they were not above using their troops to fight among themselves or with regular politicians. Carranza usually favored the army officers, particularly if the military situation in an area was shaky. Otherwise, he threw his support behind civilians—his real preference.

To ensure political order, Carranza built the most powerful military establishment Mexico had ever seen. The army's strength usually hovered around 160,000 men. The troops were well paid and benefited from Carranza's efforts to give them the best equipment possible. Carranza established the Mexican Air Force and the new war industry was manufacturing airplanes by 1918. From a variety of sources in Europe, Asia, and the United States, Carranza purchased several ships for the navy. The military particularly admired Carranza for the newly established arms industry, which was capable of manufacturing a million cartridges a day.

Opponents of Carranza, therefore, had to contend with the institutional power and self-confidence of the army, which went about its tasks with machine-like efficiency. A typical communiqué dispatched to Mexico City characteristically noted that after local troops defeated a particular band the captured rebels had all been shot on the spot.[38]

Civilian support was crucial. Carranza demanded that forces guilty of atrocities, cattle thefts, or any other abuses be punished immediately.[39] Carranza's forces seemed better disciplined than the forces they fought against. The army also received the aid of numerous villagers who wrote to Carranza to urge the retention of particularly popular army officers. Other villages made the army's tasks easier by asking for arms from the government in order to defend themselves from enemy attacks.[40]

The army shared much of the popularity of the president because it often championed popular reforms at decisive moments. The army often distributed land from seized haciendas, intervened in government to the advantage of workers, and supported Carranza's popular foreign policy. Unfortunately, army leaders acquired security and comfort that corrupted the convictions of several after 1918; and there were occasions when troops mutinied to protest the growing slowness of Treasury officials in paying them. Even with these blemishes on the record, the army never lost the prestige it had acquired during the hard struggles of 1914 to 1917.

Carranza's downfall resulted from a variety of causes. For one thing, the government's early interest in land reform and support for the working class tapered off after 1918. It was also clear by then that hopes for continued advances in school construction and a large reduction in the number of illiterates would not be realized, largely because of Carranza's fatal trust in the local governments to carry out such vital tasks. Carranza could not be considered unpopular at this point, but his vitality seemed to be sapped by a mysterious sluggishness.

By 1920 Carranza seemed unable to head off a growing crisis. A drop in rural wages and an increasing number of strikes attested to his inability to maintain the confidence of the masses. Other danger signals began to appear. He began to favor urban middle-class groups and established property holders in the interior. Carranza also made dangerous cuts in the expensive military budget, dropping thousands of officers from active service in order to pare down outlays. Nationalists were disturbed by the last-minute courting of North American businessmen who were now being invited to invest in Mexico. Exiles in the United States sent increasingly larger forces across the border to harass Carranza's northern outposts. Even Villa won a few victories, and Zapata's guerrillas were still a force to be reckoned with.

The spark that finally set off the revolt against Carranza began with a dispute over who would be his successor as president. As the generals sat down with Carranza to hammer out agreements during the campaign that culminated in the 1920 presidential elections, Carranza made his most disastrous political error—handpicking and publicly supporting the colorless Ignacio Bonillas. Bonillas, ambassador to the United States, was, of course, not even in Mexico when Carranza chose him to be his successor. Although Carranza was correct in believing that the country would support a civilian candidate, he was wrong in his choice because everyone feared that Bonillas, who had never been more than a generally unknown official, would become a puppet of Carranza.

The leader who decided to oppose Carranza was Gen. Alvaro Obregón. Obregón, the nation's best general, had never been defeated on the battlefield. He was also popular and known for his keen wit. Obregón clearly expected—and probably deserved—to be elevated to the presidency in 1920, on the basis of his popularity and military achievements.[41] Carranza, however, had always felt that Obregón would be a poor statesman, that he could not gear economic development within a strongly nationalist context. Carranza particularly feared that Obregón would abandon Carranza's independent policies and sell out to the United States. Nevertheless, Obregón had powerful support among labor, the army, and the legislature when he announced his candidacy on June 1, 1919.

Carranza responded by harassing his campaign as much as possible, arresting Obregón on trumped-up charges of treason and threatening to overturn the elections in Obregón's native Sonora. The Sonorans revolted and proclaimed the Plan de Agua Prieta. Most of the generals joined in, and Carranza was forced to flee the capital.

Carranza attempted to head east and rally his supporters from Veracruz as he had done in 1915. When rebels derailed his train and defeated the small forces still loyal to him in the mountains of Puebla, Carranza took to the hills, determined to fight to the bitter end. The government's local commander entrusted Carranza's safety to Rodolfo Herrero, a frustrated rebel who had recently surrendered to local Carranza forces. Pledging his loyalty to the harried Carranza, Herrero placed the now reduced presidential party in a few small huts in Tlaxcalantongo, Puebla.

A few days later, Herrero treacherously carried out Carranza's assassination on May 21, 1920. It was the only time when a constitutional president of Mexico was killed while holding office. For a time, both Herrero and the new government of Obregón's supporters tried to maintain the fiction that Carranza committed suicide. This story was difficult to support when the public learned that Carranza had received five bullets in various parts of his body. Although no one has ever revealed who ordered Carranza's death, it was a widespread belief at the time that Obregón had arranged it.[42] Many were shaken by the unexpected violence on the life of the country's controversial but respected leader.

Buried in a third-class grave in Mexico City, Carranza was ignored until his remains were deposited in the crypt of the Monument to the Revolution in 1942. This belated honor for Carranza was another show of unity as Mexico entered World War II on the side of the United States, an event that would have once been inconceivable.

The year 1940 represents the end of the Mexican Revolution because regimes after this year emphasized political order and industrialization rather than the Revolution's mandate for social justice; it was fitting that Carranza was reburied with respect since he defined many of the ideological goals of the Mexican Revolution that have dominated Mexico's history in the twentieth century. The Carranza epoch represented significant social changes that transformed the concept and structure of the modern Mexican state. The struggle to impose a new social order was violent and bloody, resulting in widespread suffering. Despite the obstacles, the Carranza government inaugurated firm programs toward reconstruction even as the war veterans hobbled home.

The ideology that Carranza articulated was an ardent nationalism aimed at social unity based upon reforms that benefited the masses. Responding to shortages of food, clothing, and tranquillity that confronted the country from 1914 to 1916, Carranza's populist response was realistic and politically successful.

Because of his social reforms and attractive nationalistic ideology that ushered in a new era, the government could proclaim itself the interpreter of the national will. There can be no doubt that the traditionally conservative social sectors were weakened to the point that the old upper class no longer influenced society as it once had. Carranza responded to a rising tide of class conflict by playing the dominant political role. He refused to allow his authority to be usurped by revolutionaries who did not enter into his alliance. For the first time, the political economy of Mexico distributed wealth on a wider scale while strengthening the role of the state.

Carranza restored production levels by means of strong state intervention into the traditionally export-oriented Mexican economy. Regulation of mining, petroleum, and the banks achieved more power for the state while the masses gained a better standard of living.

Carranza rallied mass support in the early years of the Revolution by means of an army of desperately poor urban and rural insurgents. This army made the task of defeating such charismatic rivals as Villa and Zapata possible, although at the cost of tragic conflict. Carranza also fought off foreign intervention and a strong conservative challenge to the Revolution after taking power.

To many, Carranza seemed to care more for Mexico than Mexicans as his government wore on. Mass political mobilization was a phenomenon that continued to make its presence felt. In retrospect, it is clear that in order to surmount the crisis of 1920 he should have maintained the tempo of militant reformism that had characterized his movement. Carranza's fundamental error was probably his attempt to convince the country that class demands were sectarian and that his new order would balance the interests of all within a context of a populist democracy. When Carranza broke the rules of his political formula by attempting to impose an unpopular successor, the army revolted and overthrew the government for the last time in recent Mexican history. Carranza passed from the scene amid the violence he himself generated; but in doing so he defined the political terms that still dominate Mexican politics and society.

NOTES

1. Douglas W. Richmond, "The Venustiano Carranza Archive," *Hispanic American Historical Review* 56 (May 1976): 290–294.
2. Emiliano Zapata is portrayed brilliantly in John Womack, *Zapata and the Mexican Revolution* (New York: Knopf, 1969). Other excellent biographies of revolutionary leaders are Stanley R. Ross, *Francisco I. Madero, Apostle of Mexican Democracy* (New York: Columbia University Press, 1955), and Michael C. Meyer, *Huerta: A Political Portrait* (Lincoln: University of Nebraska Press, 1972). A good study of Carranza's rise to power is Charles C. Cumberland, *Mexican Revolution: The Constitutionalist Years* (Austin: University of Texas Press, 1972).
3. This theme is vividly illustrated in two novels by Carlos Fuentes, *La muerte de Artemio Cruz* (Mexico City: Fondo de Cultura Económica, 1962) and *La región mas transparante* (Mexico City: Fondo de Cultura Económica, 1962).
4. For a general overview of Carranza's socioeconomic reforms, see Douglas W. Richmond, "El nacionalismo de Carranza y los cambios socioeconómicos, 1915–1920," *Historia Mexicana* 26, no. 101 (July–September 1976): 107–131.
5. See William H. Beezley, "Governor Carranza and the Revolution in Coahuila," *The Americas* 33, no. 1 (October 1976): 50–61.
6. In Héctor Aguilar Camín, *La frontera nómada: Sonora y la Revolución Mexicana* (Mexico City: Siglo Veintiuno, 1977), Sonora's history is outlined with careful precision, while William H.

Beezley's *Insurgent Governor: Abraham González and the Mexican Revolution in Chihuahua* (Lincoln: University of Nebraska Press, 1972) accomplishes much the same for Chihuahua during the Madero years.

7. Venustiano Carranza to Alvaro Obregón, May 8, 1915, Centro de Estudios de Historia de México, Mexico City, Telegramas de Venustiano Carranza, Guanajuato, carpeta 1 (hereinafter cited as TVC).
8. Gen. Pablo González to Carranza, May 25, 1915, TVC, Nuevo León, carpeta 1.
9. Gen. Jacinto B. Treviño to Carranza, July 14, 1915, TVC, Nuevo León, carpeta 1.
10. Rafael Zubarán Capmany to Andrés Magallán, April 14, 1914, TVC, Chihuahua, carpeta 1.
11. In order to understand Carranza's mining legislation, consult Marvin Bernstein, *The Mexican Mining Industry, 1890–1950* (Albany: State University of New York Press, 1954). The financial aspects are covered in Antonio Manero, *La reforma bancaria en la revolución constitucionalista* (Mexico City: Instituto Nacional de Estudios Históricos de la Revolución Mexicana, 1958). The petroleum issue is surveyed in Salvador Mendoza, *La controversia del petróleo* (Mexico City: Imprenta Politécnica, 1921).
12. An example of this trend is Gov. José Siurob to Carranza, August 7, 1916, TVC, Guanajuato, carpeta 2.
13. Carranza to Obregón, April 30, 1915, TVC, Guanajuato, carpeta 1; Carranza to Obregón, May 1, 1915, TVC, Guanajuato, carpeta 1.
14. Gen. Arnulfo González to Carranza, October 27, 1916, TVC, Coahuila, carpeta 4.
15. Carranza to Gov. Ignacio C. Enríquez, March 6, 1916, TVC, Chihuahua, carpeta 1; Gen. Francisco Murguía to Carranza, July 5, 1916, TVC, Coahuila, carpeta 3.
16. Municipal president of Guanajuato to Carranza, September 25, 1916, TVC, Guanajuato, carpeta 3; Gov. Siurob to Carranza, August 5, 1916, TVC, Guanajuato, carpeta 2; L.P.P. Gavalldon to Carranza, December 5, 1916, TVC, Coahuila, carpeta 4.
17. An interesting example is J. M. Martrez, president of the Unión Mineral Mexicana, to Carranza, [undated] 1916, TVC, Guanajuato, carpeta 4.
18. Siurob to Carranza, [undated] 1916, TVC, Guanajuato, carpeta 2.
19. For a thorough discussion of educational progress in the nation as well as in Coahuila, see Andrés Osuna, *Por la escuela y por la patria* (Mexico City: Casa Unida de Publicaciones, 1943). For the vast improvement in Coahuilan education, abundant documentation exists in the Archivo General del Estado de Coahuila, especially in legajos 292 to 305 and legajos 339 to 345.
20. Siurob to Carranza, July 24, 1916, TVC, Guanajuato, carpeta 2.
21. For a good chronology of the events, see E. Victor Niemeyer, Jr., *Revolution at Querétaro: The Mexican Constitutional Convention of 1916–1917* (Austin: University of Texas Press, 1974).

22. An excellent conceptual analysis of the role of the masses and political ideology is in Arnaldo Córdova, *La ideología de la Revolución Mexicana* (Mexico City: Ediciones Era, 1973).
23. A. Apodoca to Carranza, October 29, 1916, TVC, Colima, carpeta 2. All translations from Spanish in this essay are mine.
24. Gov. Pablo A. de la Garza to Carranza, September 9, 1916, TVC, Nuevo León, carpeta 2.
25. Carranza to Obregón, April 24, 1915, TVC, Guanajuato, carpeta 1.
26. Municipal president of Guanajuato to Carranza, September 25, 1916, TVC, Guanajuato, carpeta 3.
27. Four León, Guanajuato, miners to Carranza, February 19, 1916, Centro de Estudios de Historia de México, Mexico City, Manuscritos de don Venustiano Carranza (hereinafter cited as AC); Carranza to Gen. Cecilio García, March 7, 1916, TVC, Guanajuato, carpeta 2; Gen. Fernando Dávila to Carranza, December 27, 1916, TVC, Guanajuato, carpeta 3.
28. Carranza to ABC ministers, May 2, 1914, Archivo Histórico Diplomatico Mexicano de la Secretaría de Relaciones Exteriores de México, Mexico City, exp. LE-1579, p. 29 (hereinafter cited as AREM).
29. Statement issued by the Foreign Relations Secretariat, in *ABC*, June 17, 1914.
30. *El Pueblo*, August 26, 1915.
31. Zubarán Capmany, quoted in *El Dictamen*, August 20, 1915.
32. Zubarán Capmany to Isidro Fabela, April 17, 1914, TVC, Chihuahua, carpeta 1.
33. An excellent source for understanding these and other diplomatic confrontations is Robert Freeman Smith, *The United States and Revolutionary Nationalism in Mexico, 1916–1932* (Chicago: University of Chicago Press, 1972). Other good studies of Carranza's diplomacy are Mark T. Gilderhus, *Diplomacy and Revolution: U.S.-Mexican Relations under Wilson and Carranza* (Tucson: University of Arizona Press, 1977), and Eduardo Luquín, *La política internacional de la revolución constitucionalista* (Mexico City: Instituto Nacional de Estudios Históricos de la Revolución Mexicana, 1957).
34. Carranza to Mario Palma, March 6, 1915, TVC, Guanajuato, carpeta 1.
35. Gen. Cosío Robelo to Carranza, October 21, 1914, AC; Saltillo professor to Carranza, May 7, 1915, AC; J. G. Nava to Carranza, October 15, 1915, AREM, LE-794:88-R-31, p. 79.
36. Carranza to Gen. Antonio Medina, February 9, 1916, TVC, Guanajuato, carpeta 2.
37. Gen. Manuel M. Diéguez to Carranza, December 12, 1917, TVC, Coahuila, carpeta 5.
38. Siurob to Carranza, June 25, 1916, TVC, Guanajuato, carpeta 2.
39. Treviño to Carranza, July 9, 1915, TVC, Nuevo León, carpeta 1, Carranza to Gen. J. Espinosa y Córdoba, February 28, 1916, TVC, Guanajuato, carpeta 2.

40. War Department report to Carranza, August 7, 1918, AC; 503 residents of Jaral de Progreso to Carranza, [June ?] 1918, Guanajuato, carpeta 3.
41. For the political atmosphere surrounding Carranza's fall, see John W. F. Dulles, *Yesterday in Mexico: A Chronicle of the Revolution, 1919–1936* (Austin: University of Texas Press, 1961).
42. Examples of the literature on Carranza's assassination are Julia Carranza, *La verdad sobre la muerte de Carranza* (San Antonio, 1920); Martín Luis Guzmán, *Muertes históricos* (Mexico City: Compañía General de Ediciones, 1970); Ignacio Suárez G., *Carranza, forjador del México actual* (Mexico City: B. Costa-Amic, 1965); Francisco L. Urquizo, *Asesinato de Carranza* (Mexico City: Populibros "La Prensa," 1969); Fernando Benítez, *El rey viejo* (Mexico City: Fondo de Cultura Económica, 1959).

Obregón: Mexico's Accommodating President

DAVID C. BAILEY

ALVARO OBREGON (1880–1928), rancher, mechanic, businessman, soldier, hero of the Revolution, president of Mexico. The "happy man with one arm"[1] lies buried in the state of Sonora, a thousand miles from the hulking monument in Mexico City that guards the tombs of Francisco Madero, Venustiano Carranza, Pancho Villa, Plutarco Elías Calles, and Lázaro Cárdenas. Obregón's separation in death from those men is appropriate. They became legends, a status he never quite attained. Madero towers as the democratic visionary; Carranza stands peerless as the champion of Mexican nationalism; Villa, in the popular imagination, personifies the exploited masses in arms; Calles implemented the machinery of party government on a national basis; and Cárdenas is lionized for his zealous devotion to social justice and national dignity.

Obregón's legacy is of a different order. Beyond question he was a nationalist, and he probably believed in democracy, the rule of law, and justice for Mexico's disinherited poor. He proclaimed those goals again and again, but he believed that they were means as well as ends and that they could be modified or postponed in the interest of practical necessity. He was the great compromiser of Mexico's time of troubles, and compromise is not the stuff of which myths are made. Nevertheless, the homage that Mexican officialdom accords him is not misplaced; more than anyone of his generation, he made possible the consolidation of the political and social system that prevails in Mexico today.

This statement refers to the Obregón of the 1920s, for his career was divided into two phases. Had he died during the violent decade of the teens—as he almost did when an artillery shell from Villa's army shattered his right arm—his place in the revolutionary pantheon would be secure but secondary. Although he was a consummate military commander and a proponent of social change, he was not the leader of a faction contending for domination of the country. Obregón survived nearly all the chief actors in the great drama, except Calles, and became a bridge to the future. It fell to him to bring order out of chaos—a chaos that he had helped to create.

His early career foreshadowed only dimly the role he would later play.[2] Born into a Sonora family of respectable status but limited financial means, Obregón received a rudimentary education and rose to local prominence through hard work and inventiveness. He did not participate in the rebellion against Porfirio Díaz; but in 1912, after being elected mayor of Huatabampo, he organized a unit of state irregulars that helped quell Pascual Orozco's uprising against the Madero government. The next year he joined Carranza's movement that challenged Victoriano Huerta's usurpation. By 1914, his military talents had made the talented Sonoran a paragon of the Constitutionalist cause.

Within the revolutionary camp Obregón preferred to be a conciliator; but when events forced his hand he was a blunt partisan. Unable to mediate the conflict between Carranza and Villa, he threw his support to the First Chief; and, in a series of battles during the spring and summer of 1915, he destroyed Villa's capacity to determine Mexico's destiny. As the Constitutionalist movement grew, Obregón emerged as a social activist and helped persuade Carranza that victory depended on attracting popular support by espousing reform and practicing class politics.

During the fighting, first against Huerta and then against Villa, Obregón mounted verbal and physical assaults against enemies that he lumped together as "the reaction." He outraged businessmen by levying forced loans on them and by befriending anarchosyndicalists.[3] Branding the clergy a "malignant tumor," he held priests and bishops for ransom and confiscated places of worship.[4]

Obregón drew the wrath of foreign governments and their nationals by rejecting their demands for protection and guarantees.[5] Probably his animosity toward them was motivated more by expediency than conviction. He perceived those opponents to be the targets of imminent military attack and acted accordingly; but his early intransigence earned him a reputation as an extremist and at times this led Carranza to overrule him.[6] Still, his combativeness and his partisanship made Obregón a mentor of the activists who wrote sweeping reform provisions into the Constitution of 1917.[7]

Unwilling to challenge Carranza for the supreme leadership, Obregón withdrew from public life in 1917. But retirement would only be temporary. He was thirty-seven years old, Carranza's term as president would expire in 1920, and he waited his turn. His military prestige and his identification with popular causes gave Obregón a power base that no other revolutionary could match, a source of strength that all but guaranteed him the presidency. At the same time, Obregón's record offered little indication that he would end the strife between the revolutionary government and its opponents or among the revolutionists themselves. Only events proved otherwise.

As Carranza's rule neared its end the Revolution appeared to be stalemated. Popular aspirations awakened by Madero and encouraged by the Constitutionalists remained unsatisfied. The hacienda still dominated the countryside, and a small but militant labor movement, after having its hopes awakened, had been restrained in the name of order and higher national priorities.[8]

Meanwhile, discontent undermined the authority of a shaky government. Remnants of the Villa and Zapata movements continued their marauding, and Manuel Paláez still held much of the Veracruz coastal plain under tribute. Carranza wrestled ineffectually with the problems of national dislocation and the continual menace of intervention by the United States—the military alone consumed two-thirds of the federal budget in 1920.[9] Further, some Mexicans resented what they believed to be Carranza's lack of commitment to the ideals proclaimed in the new constitution, while others saw in the new government only the threat of radicalism.

The traditional interests—large landowners, entrepreneurs, the clergy, and foreign investors—remained hostile. Later revolutions in other countries undertook to destroy such adversaries. In Mexico, given the time and circumstances, such an uprooting was probably impossible; but, more to the point, no leader of importance advocated this action. Carranza, like Madero, insisted that special interests cooperate with the state for the national good. When cooperation was refused, the result was a standoff. Retreat was unthinkable, advance was blocked, and to stand still meant acceptance of an endless cycle of political instability, economic disorder, and foreign intimidation. Such was the prospect in 1920.

Obregón sought a way out of the dilemma. He reassured spokesmen for the masses that he was their ally, while at the same time working to persuade the Revolution's enemies that they had more to gain by accepting the new regime than by combatting it. He was, of course, the immediate beneficiary of this strategy; but he also set directions that became second nature to his successors and guaranteed the survival of Mexico's new order.

Obregón's announcement of his candidacy in June 1919, was narrowly political and broadly conciliatory. He neatly divided all Mexicans into two parties, "conservative" and "liberal." He offered himself as the candidate of the latter, which he defined to include workers, the middle class, and, in fact, everyone who contributed to the nation's material advancement. He was not magnanimous in his references to the conservative party, but he avoided vituperation; reactionaries were not mortal enemies to be destroyed, but rather political foes who could be controlled by political means.[10]

An appeal for unity, however, was not enough to assure Obregón's peaceful accession to power. Carranza's determination to keep him from the presidency by imposing his own successor—a move that stemmed, apparently, from personal animosity—triggered violence. A brief and successful insurrection led by Adolfo de la Huerta and Plutarco Elías Calles drove Carranza from office in May 1920 and cleared the way for Obregón's landslide election victory several weeks later.[11] It was an inauspicious beginning, but it did not deter him from his goal of national reconciliation.

Obregón's politics of accommodation took form in his year-long election campaign and became tangible when he entered the presidency. He courted labor and agrarian groups while assuring entrepreneurs and *hacendados* of his modera tion and sympathy. He attempted to placate Catholics but also assured anticlericals that he would maintain stern vigilance over the clergy. He curried favor with the United States government and foreign investors but avoided an explicit surrender of Mexican sovereignty. He sought unity among all Mexicans who considered themselves revolutionaries.

In his bid for the highest office, Obregón relied heavily on the support of urban labor, an old ally that had contributed the famous Red Battalions to help make possible his victory over Villa. He cemented labor's allegiance with a secret pact that promised the Confederación Regional Obrera Mexicana (CROM) and its ambitious boss, Luis N. Morones, a voice in his government.[12]

After he assumed the presidency, labor leaders received appointments to such powerful posts as the governorship of the Federal District and the head of the national armaments and munitions factory.[13] In the benevolent atmosphere of Obregón's term, CROM's membership grew from 50,000 to 1,200,000.[14] Delegates to labor conventions traveled free on government rail passes, and labor leaders in government positions were allowed to use their posts to promote organizational efforts.[15]

On the other hand, Obregón moved to ease the anxieties of businessmen, both Mexican and foreign. In a well-publicized speech in Mazatlán in November 1919, he said that "the best government will be the one that establishes an equilibrium between [capital and labor] so that on a basis of equity they will obtain the concessions that each ought to have." He emphasized increased productivity rather than redistribution of wealth. "We gain nothing by giving felt hats and shoes to those who wear straw hats and sandals," said Obregón, "if we take them away from people who have them, in the name of an equality that will set us back a century."[16]

Throughout the labor disputes of his administration, his preferred tactic was to make state governments responsible for mediation, thereby allowing him to maintain an appearance of impartiality. The syndicates won dozens of strikes every year; but in conflicts involving industries that were foreign owned or that had an important impact on the nation's economy or whose hostility could undermine his political position, Obregón intervened on the side of capital.

When Veracruz fishermen struck in 1922, he criticized the state's governor for ordering the company not to hire non-union workers to replace the strikers, noting that the constitution prohibited monopolies of any kind.[17] When striking members of the Unión Mineral Mexicana in Coahuila were fired on and killed by soldiers and laborers in the company union at the United States–owned Compañía Mineral during a protest march in 1923, Obregón blamed the victims for their intransigence and for not avoiding the clash. Thoroughly intimidated, the union collapsed.[18] During a strike at the giant El Aguila Petroleum Company in 1924, Obregón ordered local authorities to eject occupying workers from the refineries. He insisted that he disapproved of hiring scab labor; but when El Aguila did so he took no action, and the strike ended. His refusal to confront the company was evidently motivated by a fear of losing tax revenues and undoubtedly by a desire to dissuade the oil companies from supporting the Adolfo de la Huerta rebellion that threatened to topple his government.[19]

By the end of his term, Mexican labor was understandably skeptical of Obregón's friendship; but it had gained an overriding advantage, the recognition of its right to a voice in national policy making. Business interests, for their part, were not happy. They would have to contend with a labor movement whose existence appeared to be permanent; but business interests also had begun to realize that the new rules of the game allowed profit seekers a reasonable chance to prosper. Domestic and foreign trade increased steadily during Obregón's tenure, and there were impressive advances in manufacturing and construction.[20]

In his approach to the land question, Obregón followed a similar path of balancing conflicting interest. He befriended the followers of Emiliano Zapata, which established his credentials as a friend of agrarian reform and also ended the chronic rebellion in Morelos. The *zapatistas*, even before their leader's death in 1919, had eyed Obregón as a possible patron and they correctly interpreted his announcement of candidacy as a sympathetic overture.[21] When Obregón fled south to escape arrest at the climax of his electoral campaign in 1920, they rallied to him. Supporters from Morelos served as escort when he reentered Mexico City in May.

A month later, Zapata's Liberating Army of the South became part of the national military establishment, and its chief leaders, Gildardo Magaña and Genovevo de la O, received commissions as generals.[22] Under Obregón's approving eye, veteran *zapatista*, Antonio Díaz Soto y Gama, founded the National Agrarian party, some of whose leaders in Congress quickly rose to dominant positions.[23] Obregón also named Antonio Villarreal, another agrarian activist, secretary of agriculture. A series of laws and decrees confirmed land reform in Morelos, which was not at peace under *zapatista* control.[24] In 1921, on the second anniversary of Zapata's death, cabinet ministers and federal deputies attended ceremonies at the grave in Cuautla.[25] The Zapata myth had been securely launched, and Obregón shared its aura.

He had, of course, no intention of redistributing land on a grand scale. Obregón knew that the landowning class, although shorn of most of its political power, still controlled production of agricultural goods for export and an important share of the domestic food supply. To badger landowners would only worsen conditions in the already emaciated rural sector and give *hacendados* cause to back seditious movements. At the same time that he was courting *zapatistas*, Obregón addressed the Jalisco Chamber of Commerce in 1919, informing the landowners that the fundamental agrarian problem was not land tenure but productivity. It would be a mistake, he said, to destroy the haciendas before first establishing a workable system of small private holdings. He opposed creating such holdings by taking land from haciendas that used modern methods, that were demonstrably productive, and that raised crops that could be profitably marketed. He added, pointedly, that the great majority of Mexicans did not yet have the knowledge to work small individual parcels.[26]

The Jalisco chamber was euphoric. It published the address with the antiredistribution phrases in bold print and noted, in a preface to a fifth edition in 1922, that the speech had been taken as "a shield against agrarian excesses and as a guarantee of salvation for the nation's agriculture . . . a solemn promise that the right of property will be respected . . . a program not of destruction but of agricultural evolution."[27] Obregón went even further. He told a committee of Congress just before he took office that Mexico had much tillable land not being used, and that small private parcels should be formed from that source.[28]

During his presidency, Obregón followed a course in agrarian matters that produced maximum political advantage while antagonizing as few people as possible. Land redistribution totaled around three million acres[29]—eight times as much as during Carranza's term—but it was highly selective, designed not to frighten landowners, arouse the ire of foreigners, or reduce revenues in the crucial export sector. In only two states, Morelos and Yucatán, was there wholesale redistribution.[30] In Morelos, most of the haciendas had been abandoned during the Zapata rebellion, and the sugar industry was already in ruins. Around one quarter of the state's area was transferred to the villages, thereby fulfilling Zapata's aims. The adverse effect on the economy was negligible, and the government scored a net political gain. One-fifth of Yucatán's land surface was divided, but the tax-producing henequen zone was not touched. The radical Yucatán socialist movement and its leader, Felipe Carrillo Puerto, were somewhat consoled by this halfway measure and the *hacendados* remained quiescent.

In the north, the only major expropriation was the million-acre Terreno de Paloma holding in Chihuahua and Sonora. Obregón justified his seizure of the land by invoking national security, claiming that the territory was a haven for bandits who raided along the border and sometimes caused problems with United States authorities. The move was relatively safe for another reason because titles to the haciendas had long been in dispute, and the various claimants were in weak positions to oppose seizure.[31]

Few expropriations involved land held by foreigners. For example, the vast holdings of William Randolph Hearst were left intact; and Hearst, after a 1921 visit to Mexico during which Obregón extended the visitor special courtesies, praised the president for respecting property rights and for his sensible, law-abiding policies.[32]

The Church question was particularly vexing. Obregón could not defuse Catholic hostility toward him. Memories of his depredations during the armed struggle were still vivid, and animosity between Catholic leaders and revolutionists was too deep and widespread to permit any rapid change. Obregon's approach was to try to persuade the Church hierarchy, and especially the Holy See, that the government of Mexico could be flexible. So long as the clergy did not defy civil authority, he explained, he would tolerate Catholic activity beyond the limits set in the constitution. Obregón exchanged greetings with Pope Pius XI when the latter was elected to the papacy in 1922,[33] and he maintained cordial relations with the apostolic delegate.[34] The Sonoran president took no steps to thwart the growth of Catholic labor and social action groups, and he periodically reproved local anticlericals for harassing Catholics.[35]

Obregón reacted swiftly to any clerical challenge, however, going so far as to expel the papal representative for participating in a public religious ceremony. He also dispersed a eucharistic congress that was at least semipublic in nature.[36] At the same time, however, he capped his search for religious peace by concluding an agreement with the Vatican in 1924. By its terms, Mexico agreed to allow a new apostolic delegate to reside in the country in exchange for Rome's pledge to appoint as bishops only Mexican priests who abstained from political activity.[37]

When Calles, Obregón's successor, broke the truce by pressing for confrontation with the Church, Obregón privately disapproved of the policy and conducted quiet negotiations with the clergy in an effort to reach a new settlement.[38] After his reelection in 1928, Obregón was preparing new initiatives to end the conflict when, ironically, he was killed by a young Catholic zealot.[39]

Relations with the United States tested to its furthest limits Obregón's skill at compromise. Washington had never admitted Mexico's claim, stipulated in the 1917 Constitution, to absolute sovereignty over surface and subsoil properties, many of which were held by foreigners. The United States recognized Carranza's government only reluctantly and, suspending relations with Mexico when Carranza was overthrown, decided to force the new regime to repudiate the offensive laws as the price for resuming normal diplomatic ties.

Obregón tried to evade the issue. He gave repeated verbal assurances of his friendship, telling the United States chargé d'affaires, for example, that he believed Carranza's anti-United States policies had been a mistake. He proposed a Pan

American front, to be headed by the United States, against future threats from Europe or the Orient.[40] He told the United States press, as well as the Foreign Chamber of Commerce in Mexico City, that Mexico needed and welcomed foreign capital to aid national reconstruction.[41]

Words, however, were not enough. Washington decided to withhold recognition until Obregón agreed to nullify the provisions of the constitution that applied to foreign holdings. This decision amounted to a demand that Mexico renounce its right to legislate over nearly half of its natural wealth.[42]

Obregón managed to avoid enshrining surrender in a treaty, as the United States at first insisted he must; but ultimately he met most of the demands. In a 1921 decision on a case involving petroleum rights and in subsequent rulings, the Mexican Supreme Court held that Article 27 of the constitution, which declared that all subsoil deposits were the property of the nation, did not apply to companies and individuals that had acquired their titles before 1917 and that by "positive acts" had made clear their intentions to exploit their holdings.[43]

Washington was unimpressed, and Obregón escalated his efforts. In 1922, he authorized an agreement with the International Committee of Bankers on Mexico that acknowledged debt obligations to foreigners amounting to a staggering billion and a half pesos. He hoped this would placate Washington and also clear the way for the granting of desperately needed credit; but credit was not forthcoming, and neither was diplomatic recognition.

In a final, desperate move—the Bucareli Agreements of August 1923—Obregón pledged executive backing of the court rulings on retroactivity and agreed to the establishment of mixed commissions to adjudicate claims for losses incurred by United States citizens and corporations, both before and during the Revolution. He insisted that the accords in no way sacrificed principle, a rationalization that satisfied only his staunchest supporters at the time and few students of the question afterward. It was a victory nonetheless. Washington granted the coveted recognition, foreign loans and investments began to flow in, and Obregón's ready access to United States military equipment during the rebellion that erupted against him three months later probably saved his regime.

The accommodation with the United States was a watershed in the foreign relations of governments emanating from the Revolution. For the next fifteen years there were periodic disputes with Washington, culminating in the 1938 crisis over Mexico's expropriation of foreign oil companies; but official relations between the two countries were never interrupted again. United States investments were welcome and profitable and, as Obregón had intended, became a main ingredient of national economic growth.

Success in maintaining a popular image while mollifying the special interests gave Obregón's government a stability that none had enjoyed in Mexico for many years. His achievements, however, would have counted for nothing if he had not dealt successfully with a menace that haunted him from the start. The Revolution had created a climate of violence, and thousands of Mexicans remained under arms. Many of them were nominally a part of the national army. Others were formally outside the law. All of them followed impulsive and ambitious chieftains who had grown accustomed to deciding for themselves how to use the might they commanded. Some of these leaders were old associates of Obregón's; others were sworn enemies. Some, like Pancho Villa, were in eclipse but still possessed the capability to cause trouble. Others dreamed of glories yet to come. To discipline such a horde was both difficult and dangerous.

Pacifying Villa was relatively uncomplicated, if expensive. From his lair in the north, Villa had earlier volunteered to join the rebellion against Carranza, an offer that Obregón's associates evidently declined. After the old chief's death, Villa expressed a desire to lay down his arms in exchange for certain guarantees. The negotiations languished; but after Villa led a brief, but damaging, foray into Coahuila in the summer of 1920 Interim President Adolfo de la Huerta came to terms. The government purchased for Villa's use a 25,000-acre hacienda in Durango for more than a half million pesos, granted him permission to maintain a large bodyguard, and awarded him an annual subsidy.[44]

Obregón, who at first opposed the amnesty, honored it nevertheless and spared no effort or cost to keep Villa happy and quiet. He increased the payments to more than a hundred thousand pesos a year; and Villa, until his death in 1923, enjoyed direct access to the president, who treated him with studied courtesy and apparently developed a certain fondness for his old foe.[45]

In dealing with the regular army, whose freebooting contingents numbered perhaps a hundred thousand men in 1920,[46] Obregón had the advantage of personal popularity. When his presidential campaign ended in revolt, he had the support of key military leaders and most of the rank and file. Loyalty was tentative, however, in a conglomerate commanded by more than five hundred generals, many of whom had large personal followings and whose thirst for political preferment was at least as great as Obregón's. The president singled out some of them for special attention. Plutarco Elías Calles, the only general whose instinct for mass politics approached Obregón's own, was given the top cabinet post. Others who had unusual abilities or popular appeal were also brought into the government (six of nine members of Obregón's cabinet at the start were generals) or received other generous favors. Meanwhile, Obregón discharged nearly half of the army and gave them inducements to become law-abiding civilians.[47]

When cooption failed, Obregón met force with force and seized the opportunity to discourage military excursions into politics. Conspiracies hatched in 1921 and 1922, mainly by friends of the dead Carranza, were quickly snuffed out and their instigators executed.[48] Far more serious was the rebellion mounted in December 1923, which was led by Adolfo de la Huerta and joined by almost half the army.

In that crisis, the fruits of Obregón's politics of accommodation were impressively apparent. Only a handful of landowners and businessmen sided with the rebels; Catholic leaders stayed neutral. The United States expedited arms shipment to the government, and Luis Morones and the CROM mobilized all their resources to combat the insurrection. With his flanks secure, Obregón took the field in person and crushed the uprising in a matter of weeks. He punished captured rebel officers without mercy and bountifully rewarded those who had remained loyal.[49]

It was the last time that his government or any that followed it was in real danger of being overthrown by the Mexican Army. Residual attempts over the next dozen years lacked both expert direction and popular support. Henceforth, generals who succeeded in gaining high political office did so by building civilian followings and submitting themselves to the electoral process. After 1924 the only Mexican general who might have imposed himself by force was Obregón, and by then he had no need of such methods. He stood alone.

The most striking thing about the career of Alvaro Obregón was his personal success. Of all the luminaries of the Revolution only he ended his life as the master of Mexico. His reelection to the presidency in 1928 was pro forma despite its contravention of the principle of no reelection, the cry under which Francisco Madero had launched his revolt against Porfirio Díaz eighteen years earlier. It seems probable that only Obregón's death at the hands of an assassin spared Mexico a new era of one-man rule. His abilities were adequate to his ambition. His talent for compromise, his skill at convincing mutually hostile groups that he was their benefactor, his occasional ruthlessness and his personal magnetism all fit the familiar profile of the caudillo that he indeed was. To leave the story at that, however, is only to add one more example to the long list of strongman triumphs in Mexican and Latin American history. More important is what his success reveals about the Mexico of his time and about the Mexican Revolution.

In large part, Obregón prevailed because so many Mexicans were willing that he should. For most of them the Revolution was over. After a decade of strife, much of it inconclusive, compromise was welcome. Scattered rebel bands were weakened by exhaustion and feelings of futility; their chiefs persuaded them—and themselves—that Obregón represented a hope for justice and security. The anarchy of the teens had receded, and groups that deplored the Revolution and had feared doom at its hands were, in most cases, ready to resume life under reduced but bearable circumstances. The soldiers and politicians that the years of turmoil had thrown up—the embryonic "Revolutionary Family"—were more eager to join the old elites than to dislodge them, and the new prosperity offered ample opportunity.

The Obregón years witnessed a rebirth of hope in which innovation was more a challenge than a threat. The Mexican press enjoyed a degree of freedom it had seldom known before, and a galaxy of new periodicals made their appearance.

Political debate was open and raucous, if occasionally dangerous to life and limb. The educational zeal of José Vasconcelos and his colleagues in the new Ministry of Education sparked a whirlwind of activity in the countryside, where two thousand schools opened their doors between 1920 and 1925.[50] The mural art of Diego Rivera and José Clemente Orozco that began to adorn public buildings represented a cultural renaissance unequaled in Mexico's history. Obregón rode the crest of an optimism in which all things seemed possible. The expansive atmosphere gave him the opportunity to undertake initiatives that would give tangible meaning to the Revolution as he understood it.

Obregón's definitions of revolution, which he gave at various times during his fifteen years of national prominence, were so diverse as to be almost meaningless; but his actions as president indicate clearly what he believed the Revolution's goal to be. It was modernization, and by this Obregón meant Mexico's entry into the Western world of his day. He accepted as a matter of course the models and values that he believed had produced development in the United States and Europe. In this belief he did not differ markedly from Madero and Carranza, but he was able and willing to act on its practical implications for Mexico.

He embraced both capitalism and populism and accepted without hesitation the active intervention of the state to promote them. The competition of the market was a modernizing force to be encouraged, the only condition being that it benefit the Mexican collectivity as well as the investors. At the same time, in order for modernization to be real and not ephemeral he believed that all Mexicans must be brought into the process. Obregón's commitment to bettering the lot of the masses suited his sense of justice. Reform was also indispensable for national integration and political stability, both of which were components of modernization in the advanced nations that he wanted Mexico to emulate. To promote the well-being of workers and *campesinos* while supporting capital was complementary, not contradictory. His enemy was the Mexican past—a past, as he saw it, that was so pervaded by ignorance and repression that advance had been impossible. The Revolution's great work was to remove barriers, to allow and, where necessary, to mandate an equilibrium in which all would contribute to progress and all could benefit according to their contributions.

The merits of such a course were confirmed, Obregón believed, by his own experience in Sonora. He never tired of touting his success as a commercial farmer, which he attributed to his ingenuity and his understanding of markets. Although he delighted in making rhetorical sweeps about inexorable social forces, the constant theme in his speeches and writings was a stress on hard work, personal responsibility, and morality. "God never helps fools," he once remarked.[51] The Revolution did not seek to create a "new man" but, rather, modern men who would build a new country. Obregón's ambition, personal values, and plans for Mexico came together in happy harmony. His policies were self-serving, but they also served the interests, however imperfectly, of most segments of Mexican society.

In retrospect, his assessment of the Mexican reality was simplistic. He underestimated the obstacles that blocked the climb to modernity and the size of the gulf that, even in his day, separated Mexico from the few nations that had begun development. It may be argued that, in fact, the Revolution Obregón served—and that served him—was the wrong revolution for Mexico; but he did not believe so, and for long decades after his death neither did most observers of the Mexican experience. Obregón did not start the Mexican Revolution and he did not give it a distinctive ideology. Instead, he defined it in practice, and his accomplishments tell more about the nature of the Revolution than do the words and deeds of the legendary heroes whose company Obregón never joined.

NOTES

1. So called by Hudson Strode, *Timeless Mexico* (New York: Harcourt, Brace, 1944).
2. On Obregón's early life, see Djed Bórquez [pseudonym for Juan de Dios Bojórquez], *Obregón: Apuntes biográficos* (Mexico City: Ediciones Patria Nueva, 1929), and E. J. Dillon, *President Obregon—A World Reformer* (Boston: Small, Maynard, 1923).
3. *La Prensa*, February 25, March 3, 1915; Alberto Pani, *Apuntes autobiográficos*, 2 vols. (Mexico City: M. Porrúa, 1951), 1:227–

229; Alvaro Obregón, *Ocho mil kilómetros en campaña: Relación de las acciones de armas efectuadas en más de veinte estados de la República durante un periodo de cuatro años* (Mexico City, 1917), p. 270; J. M. Cardoso de Oliveira to William Jennings Bryan, March 4, 1915, file 812.00/14500, National Archives, Record Group (National Archives hereinafter cited as NA and Record Group as RG).

4. *Mexican Herald*, February 19, 1915; *La Prensa*, February 21, March 3, 1915; Obregón, *Ocho mil kilómetros*, pp. 405, 406; Francisco Orozco y Jiménez, *¡Acerquémonos a Dios! Memorándum del Arzobispo de Guadalajara* (Guadalajara, 1918), pp. 17, 18.
5. Obregón, *Ocho mil kilómetros*, pp. 280–285; Woodrow Wilson to Bryan, March 6, 1915, file 812.00/14504, NA, RG 59.
6. Obregón, *Ocho mil kilómetros*, pp. 405, 406; Subsecretario Encargado del Despacho, Secretaría de Relaciones Exteriores, Veracruz, to John R. Silliman, February 27, 1915, and Carranza to Obregón, February 25, 1915, Archivo Histórico de la Secretaría de Relaciones Exteriores, L-E-1573, exp. 70.
7. Charles C. Cumberland, *Mexican Revolution: The Constitutionalist Years* (Austin: University of Texas Press, 1972), pp. 330, 334.
8. Ibid., pp. 385–390; Ramón Eduardo Ruiz, *Labor and the Ambivalent Revolutionaries: Mexico, 1911–1923* (Baltimore: Johns Hopkins University Press, 1976), pp. 71, 72.
9. Edwin Lieuwen, *Mexican Militarism: The Political Rise and Fall of the Revolutionary Army, 1919–1940* (Albuquerque: University of New Mexico Press, 1968), p. 153.
10. "Manifiesto a la Nación, lanzada por el C. Alvaro Obregón," in José Vasconcelos, *La caída de Carranza: De la dictadura a la libertad* (Mexico City: Impr. de Murguía, 1920), pp. 3–26.
11. On the events of 1920, see Vasconcelos, *La caída de Carranza*, and Cumberland, *Mexican Revolution*, pp. 401–413.
12. Marjorie Ruth Clark, *Organized Labor in Mexico* (Chapel Hill: University of North Carolina Press, 1934), pp. 72, 73.
13. Ibid., pp. 74–78.
14. Ernest Gruening, *Mexico and Its Heritage* (New York: Century, 1928), p. 339. The figures are CROM's.
15. Frank Tannenbaum, *Peace by Revolution: Mexico after 1910* (New York: Columbia University Press, 1933), pp. 247, 248.
16. *Discursos del General Alvaro Obregón*, 2 vols. (Mexico City, 1932), 1:67. All translations from Spanish in this essay are mine.
17. Ruiz, *Labor and the Ambivalent Revolutionaries*, p. 93.
18. Ibid., pp. 89, 90.
19. Ibid., pp. 91–93.
20. See, for example, Manuel Collás and Adalberto García Rocha, "El desarrollo económico reciente de México," in *Contemporary Mexico*, ed. James W. Wilkie, Michael C. Meyer, and Edna Monzón de Wilkie (Berkeley and Los Angeles: University of California Press, 1976), pp. 405–440.

21. John Womack, *Zapata and the Mexican Revolution* (New York: Knopf, 1969), pp. 338, 339.
22. Ibid., pp. 362–364.
23. Ibid., p. 366.
24. Ibid., pp. 366–369.
25. Nemesio García Naranjo, "El mito de Zapata," *Siempre*, November 21, 1957, p. 18.
26. *El problema agrícola y agraria: Conferencia sustentada por el General Obregón en Guadalajara el 18 de noviembre de 1919*, 5th ed. (Guadalajara, 1922).
27. Ibid.
28. *El problema agrario: Versión taquigráfica del cambio de impresiones entre el presidente electo A. Obregón y un grupo de diputados en octubre de 1920* (Mexico City, 1920).
29. This amount was transferred by federal action. In addition, state and local agrarian commissions made provisional awards that often were confirmed only years later.
30. Jan Bazant, *A Concise History of Mexico: From Hidalgo to Cárdenas, 1805–1940* (New York: Cambridge University Press, 1977), p. 157.
31. Obregón decree, January 11, 1923, Archivo General de la Nación, "Archivo de los Presidentes, Obregón-Calles," 121-A-P-1 (Archivo General de la Nación hereinafter cited as AGN).
32. W. R. Hearst editorial in *New York American*, November 13, 1921, copy in AGN, "Archivo de los Presidentes, Obregón Calles," 104-R, I-E-5; W. A. Swanberg, *Citizen Hearst: A Biography of William Randolph Hearst* (New York: Scribners, 1961), p. 402.
33. Ernest Lagarde, Memorandum, in file 812.404/867 1/2, NA, RG 59.
34. Ibid.; Ernesto Filippi to Obregón, December 30, 1921; Obregón to Filippi, January 2, 1922; Filippi to Obregón, June 3, 1922, AGN, "Archivo de los Presidentes, Obregón-Calles," 417-F-1.
35. For example, Obregón to governor of Veracruz, May 2, 1923, and Obregón to Ricardo Vargas, May 2, 1923, AGN, "Archivo de los Presidentes, Obregón-Calles," 438-0-06.
36. Alicia Olivera Sedano, *Aspectos del conflicto religioso de 1926 a 1929: Sus antecedentes y consecuencias* (Mexico City: Instituto Nacional de Antropología e Historia, 1966), pp. 92, 93.
37. The agreement was contained in an exchange of letters between Aarón Sáenz, Obregón's secretary of foreign relations, and Pietro Cardinal Gasparri, the papal secretary of state. Texts may be found in Elizabeth Ann Rice, *The Diplomatic Relations between the United States and Mexico, as Affected by the Struggle for Religious Liberty in Mexico, 1925–1929* (Washington, D.C.: Catholic University of America Press, 1959), pp. 199–201.
38. Miguel Alessio Robles, "Obregón como político y militar," *Todo*, August 5, 1943, p. 7; David C. Bailey, *¡Viva Cristo Rey! The Cristero Rebellion and the Church-State Conflict in Mexico* (Austin: University of Texas Press, 1974), pp. 157–160.
39. Dwight W. Morrow to secretary of state, July 23, 1928, file 812.404/895 2/9, NA, RG 59.

40. George T. Summerlin to Charles M. Johnson, chief, Division of Mexican Affairs, June 1, 1920, file 711.12/531, NA, RG 59.
41. *Excélsior*, September 14, November 29, 1920.
42. See Frank Tannenbaum, *Mexico: The Struggle for Peace and Bread* (New York: Knopf, 1950), pp. 266, 267.
43. The complex negotiations that finally resulted in U.S. recognition are summarized in Charles W. Hackett, *The Mexican Revolution and the United States, 1910–1926*, World Peace Foundation Pamphlets, 9, no. 5 (Boston, 1926), pp. 339–446. John W. F. Dulles, *Yesterday in Mexico: A Chronicle of the Revolution, 1919–1936* (Austin: University of Texas Press, 1961), also analyzes the settlement and surveys a portion of the literature on the controversy.
44. Dulles, *Yesterday in Mexico*, pp. 68–70.
45. Obregón's relations with Villa after 1920 are documented in part in the AGN, "Secretaría Particular de la Presidencia de la República," 101-V-3, leg. 22.
46. Adolfo de la Huerta, "Informe rendido . . . ante el H. Congreso de la Unión," September 1, 1920, *Diario Oficial* 16 (Mexico City, 1920): 32.
47. Lieuwen, *Mexican Militarism*, p. 67.
48. Ibid., pp. 63, 64.
49. Ibid., p. 78; Dulles, *Yesterday in Mexico*, pp. 258–263.
50. Bazant, *A Concise History of Mexico*, p. 163.
51. Djed Bórquez, "Presencia de Obregón," *Así*, July 22, 1944, p. 13.

Cárdenas: Creating a Campesino Power Base for Presidential Policy

LYLE C. BROWN

DURING the period from 1934 to 1940, Gen. Lázaro Cárdenas won the presidency, freed himself from the tutelage of Gen. Plutarco Elías Calles, effected a necessary détente with the Catholic hierarchy, mobilized the latent political power of Mexico's *campesinos* and industrial workers, and reorganized the machinery of the Partido Nacional Revolucionario (PNR) so as to control the election of his successor. In short, he obtained political power, strengthened and maintained that power, and, finally, transferred his power after serving a full presidential term.

Throughout these years Cárdenas gave priority to the revolutionary goal of distributing land to the impoverished peasantry. At the same time he sought to weld the country's *campesino* organizations into a powerful base of political support that would make his administration less dependent upon organized labor, professional politicians, government bureaucrats, and the military. Of special significance is the fact that Cárdenas carried out his political operations with minimum use of force but under such difficult conditions that a serious error in the manipulation of peasant political mobilization might have plunged Mexico into chaos.[1]

Before his selection as presidential candidate of the PNR in 1934, Cárdenas had held important government and party positions, had been a close associate of former President Calles for nearly two decades, and had enjoyed a successful career as a popular and efficient army officer. Because of his youth and his radical tendencies, however, Cárdenas might have failed to receive Calles's endorsement had it not been for the influence of powerful pro-Cárdenas elements within the PNR.

These *cardenistas* were also responsible for the radical reform planks in the party's platform, the Six Year Plan. Although opposing parties were weak and could present no real challenge to the candidate of the PNR, Cárdenas campaigned vigorously throughout the country and emphasized his determination to carry out the promises of the PNR platform.

In 1934, shortly after Cárdenas assumed office, Mexico was convulsed by a series of strikes that resulted from interunion conflict and the president's openly expressed sympathy with labor's demands for higher wages and better working conditions. When Calles criticized the strike activities of Mexican union leaders, Cárdenas interpreted Calles's statements as criticism of the administration's labor policy. Most politicians expected that the president would defer to his patron, but Cárdenas defended his labor policy and made it abundantly clear that he would not tolerate interference.

At the same time, Cárdenas carried out a purge of *callista* deputies and cabinet members, and Calles retired to Sinaloa. When Calles returned to Mexico City at the end of 1935 and attempted to organize an opposition movement, Cárdenas ordered the reassignment of generals of dubious loyalty, caused leading *callistas* to be expelled from the PNR, and arranged a purge of pro-Calles governors and senators. Finally, in April 1936 Calles sought exile in the United States.

Realizing that education of the masses represented Mexico's most pressing need and aware of the fact that the classroom could be used as an agency for disseminating propaganda in support of his policies, Cárdenas sought to expand the country's public school system. Anticlerical and even antireligious elements of the government's socialist education program, however, provoked strong opposition from the Catholic hierarchy. Convinced that a prolonged religious conflict would interfere with other phases of his administration, Cárdenas chose to appease the clergy. He modified the educational program, used his influence to open more churches, and lifted restrictions concerning the number of priests allowed to function in the country.[2]

Shortly after the meeting of the Seventh Comintern Congress in Moscow in 1935 the Partido Communista de México (PCM) sought to create a popular front. Mexican

Communist officials soon managed to alienate both labor and PNR leaders who refused to accept PCM direction. The popular front movement in Mexico failed, even though the Communists eventually humbled themselves before their former PNR opponents in a desperate attempt to win their cooperation and thus comply with Moscow's orders.

Without giving any indication of being influenced by the PCM's popular front plan, Cárdenas called for the remodeling of the official party late in 1937, so as to create a functional organization that would consist of labor, peasant, military, and popular sectors. As a result of this move, the Partido Revolucionario Mexicano (PRM) came into existence in 1938 and provided the necessary political machinery for effecting the nomination and election of Cárdenas's successor, Gen. Manuel Avila Camacho.[3]

Cárdenas's enemies complained about his methods and others criticized his choice of objectives. None, however, could dispute the fact that he acquired political power in an impressive fashion, increased that power while at the same time implementing revolutionary reforms that invited strong opposition, and transferred his power to a successor who was nominated and elected through use of the political machinery that Cárdenas had fashioned.

In a country where the three preceding presidents had been dominated by General Calles, the Jefe Máximo of the Revolution, and where violence had become institutionalized as a political process, only a strong leader and a skillful organizer could free himself from Calles's tutelage and serve out a full six-year term as president. Cárdenas was such a man.

With the end of the most violent stage of the Mexican Revolution in 1917, tens of thousands of land-hungry troops returned home with the hope of obtaining for themselves or their villages at least a portion of the large landed estates that accounted for over half of the country's agricultural property. After all, most of the big landowners had opposed the Revolution, while even the most conservative revolutionary leaders had made some commitment to a program of land reform.

Although little land was distributed officially from 1911 to 1916, the framers of the Constitution of 1917 provided a constitutional basis for land reform in Article 27. Nevertheless, Mexico's presidents from Venustiano Carranza to Abelardo Rodríguez usually implemented this constitutional provision slowly. Impoverished, generally illiterate *campesinos*, even those who had experienced years of military service, hesitated to challenge powerful landowners protected by hired gunmen and sometimes supported by the revolutionary government's own troops. Despite discouragement and danger, land hunger motivated some organized *campesinos* to form peasant leagues for the purpose of exerting pressure on politicians for distribution of more land and for protection of their communal village lands, or *ejidos*.

Political rivalries and personal animosities, however, often resulted from the organization of two or more peasant leagues within the same area, and interleague conflicts were common. Unfortunately, most of the peasant groups became political tools manipulated by leaders who were primarily concerned with obtaining public office and enriching themselves.[4]

Attempts were made to weld all state and local peasant leagues into a single national organization. Although none actually succeeded, by March 1933 the Liga Nacional Campesina "Úrsulo Galván," named after a well-known Veracruz peasant leader who died in 1930, claimed affiliated groups in twenty-two states, while the Liga Central de Comunidades Agrarias and the Liga Nacional Campesina had fewer affiliates.[5]

The year 1933 also marked the launching of another peasant unification movement, the Confederación Campesina Mexicana (CCM), by a small group of politicians who used the organization for launching a campaign designed to secure the PNR presidential nomination for Cárdenas. According to Emilio Portes Gil, "When, in 1933, the preliminary presidential soundings were being made . . . Professor Graciano Sánchez, Enrique Flores Magón, León García, and I proceeded to organize the Confederación Campesina Mexicana by holding a convention in the city of San Luis Potosí which was attended by Leagues of Agrarian Communities of Tamaulipas, Michoacán, San Luis Potosí and Chihuahua."[6]

Subsequently, these politicians made public, on May 3, 1933, a manifesto bearing the signatures of state peasant league leaders and calling on the Liga Nacional Campesina

"Ursulo Galván" to support the candidacy of Cárdenas.[7] Labor organizations also began to indicate their preference for Cárdenas; but many veteran PNR leaders clearly leaned toward Gen. Manuel Pérez Treviño, president of the PNR.[8]

By early June, Calles had decided that Cárdenas should be the PNR candidate.[9] On June 7, Pérez Treviño announced his withdrawal from the presidential contest. Pérez Treviño explained his action by saying that a visible majority of the PNR membership had already indicated a preference for Cárdenas. He also expressed the feeling that, in view of the many economic and social problems confronting the country, it was inadvisable to allow "the development of inflammatory activities and overflowing of passions." Instead, Pérez Treviño declared that the times called for sacrifice of personal ambitions and the promotion of harmony and unity within the party. He recommended that his followers should give their unqualified support to Cárdenas.[10] Both Calles and the incumbent president, Abelardo Rodríguez, publicly lauded Pérez Treviño for his act of self-sacrifice.[11]

In December 1933, PNR delegates met in Querétaro to nominate Cárdenas and to act on a proposed party platform, the Six Year Plan. At the insistence of Graciano Sánchez and other *cardenista* delegates, the platform committee recommendation was amended to provide for the resolution of legal difficulties that had prevented many villages from obtaining lands.

The *cardenistas* also persuaded the PNR convention to call for creation of a federal agrarian department to supervise land distribution and *ejido* affairs. They succeeded in obtaining support for another plan that proposed modification of agrarian laws to ensure faster action on petitions for land, and to make peasants residing on large estates (*peones acasillados*) eligible to receive land along with peasants residing in free villages.

To supervise the administration of land reform at the state level, Sánchez and his supporters obtained approval for the proposed establishment of a three-member mixed agrarian commission for each state. The commission would be composed of representatives of the federal agrarian department, the state government, and *campesino* organizations. Furthermore, the *cardenistas* added a pledge to continue the land reform program until the needs of the villages of each region should be resolved completely.[12]

In presenting these demands, Sánchez declared that, in spite of the Revolution, the situation of the rural workers had improved very little. At the same time, he charged that donations of land were often insufficient to support the recipients, denounced widespread corruption among government officials administering the land reform program, and pointed out that large landowners frequently were able to escape the consequences of land reform laws by dividing their holdings among relatives and even among persons not related to them.[13]

Throughout his presidential campaign, Cárdenas emphasized that the principal need of Mexico was for agrarian reform that would break up large landholdings and promote the organization of *ejidos.* Insisting that this fundamental problem must be resolved before all others, he pledged that action would be taken to ensure complete satisfaction of the land needs of the villages during the first two years of his administration.[14]

Further, Cárdenas declared that his government would arm the peasants so that they could defend their *ejidos* against hostile elements. "I have always maintained that only by arming agrarian elements that have been, and always will be, the firm bulwark of the Revolution, will they be able to carry out their mission," he stated; "I shall give to the *campesinos* the Mausers with which they fought the Revolution so that they can defend themselves, the *ejido*, and the rural school."[15]

Cárdenas' support of land reform apparently struck a popular response. On July 1, 1934, Mexico's *campesinos* and others cast their ballots in the presidential election. The government announced later that Cárdenas had received nearly one hundred times as many votes as were credited to Antonio Villarreal, who led the three opposition candidates with fewer than 25,000 votes.[16]

During the five months after the presidential election, Mexico experienced several strikes as workers pressed for higher wages. The aggressive organizing activities of Vicente Lombardo Toledano's Confederación General de Obreros y

Campesinos de México (CGOCM) further contributed to labor unrest because creation of this new labor central led to interunion conflicts with the older Confederación Regional Obrera Mexicana (CROM) and the Confederación General de Trabajodores (CGT).

Following the inauguration of Cárdenas on November 31, 1934, the tempo of labor agitation accelerated. Union leaders were encouraged by the president's strong prolabor stand to press for new gains. Finally, on the morning of June 11, 1935, a group of *callista* senators traveled to Cuernavaca to confer with Calles concerning this unrest. According to one account of the meeting, prepared by Sen. Ezequiel Padilla and published by Mexico City's leading newspapers on the following day, the Jefe Máximo denounced the strikes and charged that certain labor leaders were merely "playing with the economic life of the country" in order to promote their "bastardly interests."[17]

Cárdenas reacted immediately by issuing a statement upholding the right to strike.[18] Subsequently, Calles retreated to the more peaceful rural atmosphere of his El Tambor residence in Sinaloa, and Cárdenas replaced *callistas* in his cabinet and in the PNR secretariat.[19]

Shortly after the beginning of the Cárdenas administration, Lombardo Toledano's CGOCM held its first regular congress. The congress adopted a resolution calling for the establishment of a single proletarian confederation that would embrace all urban and rural workers in the country.[20] Cárdenas, according to Lombardo Toledano, approved this unification plan.[21] When a month passed without success in implementing the plan, Cárdenas conferred with representatives of the CGOCM, CROM, and CGT, together with spokesmen for independent unions of railroads, sugar, motion picture, mining, textile, petroleum, and metallurgical workers.

On January 29, 1935, as a result of a meeting with Cárdenas, labor leaders agreed to begin unification negotiations immediately in the offices of the Alianza de Uniones y Sindicatos de Artes Gráficas.[22] Interunion strife continued to hamper unification activity, however, until June 12, when Senator Padilla publicized critical statements about strikes and labor leaders made by Calles in Cuernavaca. This development prompted representatives of the major labor organizations, except CROM and the CGT, to issue a declaration in support of Cárdenas[23] and to sign a solidarity pact establishing a National Committee of Proletarian Defense. Included among the signers were representatives of Lombardo Toledano's CGOCM and the Communist-controlled Confederación Sindical Unitaria de México (CSUM).

Under the terms of the pact, the committee would deal with interunion conflicts and would protect workers' rights by declaring a general strike if conditions should warrant. Furthermore, the committee was directed to convoke a national congress of laborers and peasants for the purpose of creating a single proletarian central organization.[24]

Although Cárdenas welcomed the support of Lombardo Toledano and other labor leaders during the crisis provoked by Calles's remarks, the president decided that they should not be allowed to undertake the unification of Mexico's *campesinos*. While in Cuautla, Morelos, on July 9, 1935, he signed a resolution (*acuerdo*) designating his own party, the PNR, as the organization having primary responsibility for creating a national peasant confederation and for proposing legislation designed to guarantee the social and economic welfare of its members. Proclaimed on July 10, this document paved the way for eventual organization of the Confederación Nacional Campesina (CNC), which would encompass more than a million peasants who could be mobilized for both military and political purposes.[25]

Although the Cárdenas resolution did not have the force of law, it was readily accepted and implemented by all Mexican functionaries who were interested in keeping their jobs. This presidential dictate asserted: "The situation in which the peasants of the Republic have been developing their social and economic life has been, in general, contrary to the objective of unification that the Mexican Revolution has desired, because in the majority of the states on many occasions the existing disorganization has caused lamentable conflicts detrimental to the national economy and has been provoked by people who have had no designs other than to satisfy personal appetites to the injury of this social sector."[26] The president also warned that "such disorganization is the principal reason why the donation and restitution of lands to the villages has been frequently interrupted to the prejudice of the rural proletariat whose needs have not been satisfied."[27] The government's agrarian reform program, Cárdenas charged, had failed in many cases because of a corrupt alliance between officials and landowners.[28]

The Cárdenas resolution, implemented under the direction of the president's political party, required that a convention be convened in each state for the purpose of organizing a single peasant league. To constitute such a convention, two delegates would be elected to represent each *ejido* or peasant locale regardless of whether they had received provisional or definitive possession of their lands. Peasant groups that had merely filed applications for the donation or restitution of lands not yet received were to be entitled to similar representation.

As soon as the new peasant leagues were organized in each state, the central executive committee of the PNR would call a national convention to create a central peasant organization. The PNR's central executive committee was also instructed to propose laws establishing systems of peasant life insurance, sickness and accident insurance, crop insurance, and other programs that might be conducive to the social and economic betterment of the members of the new organization. Finally, the resolution stipulated that the Agrarian Department and all other executive agencies of the federal and state governments would be expected to render such assistance as might be needed by the PNR in order to ensure the successful development of the project.[29]

On July 30, 1935, PNR President Emilio Portes Gil, who also served as chairman of the Organizing Committee of Peasant Unification, sent a circular to all members of the federal Congress directing them to proceed with the organizing of peasants within their districts according to the wishes of the president.[30]

About this same time, the League of Agrarian Communities of the state of Veracruz sent another circular to its affiliates advising them of the results of a recent conference, between the president and a committee headed by Adalberto Tejeda, concerning the problems of Veracruz peasants. While promising to deal justly with their problems, Cárdenas had emphasized the importance of holding a state congress on unification to establish a single peasant league within Veracruz.[31]

The first unification congress to be held following the proclamation of Cárdenas's resolution, however, convened in Mexico City on September 7. Under the supervision of the PNR's Organizing Committee of Peasant Unification, 149 delegates from agrarian communities within the Federal District gathered in the Hidalgo Theater to comply with the president's dictate. The presence of members of the Senate and Chamber of Deputies, Supreme Court justices, cabinet ministers, representatives of the diplomatic corps, high-ranking military personnel, and top PNR functionaries emphasized the importance of the affair.[32] Cárdenas was also present and delivered an address, the general content of which was to be repeated by him and his collaborators at other congresses during the following two years.[33]

Dwelling on the problems posed by the existence of rival *campesino* organizations and implying strongly that government assistance would depend in large measure on the willingness of all peasant groups to unite within a single organization, Cárdenas pointed out that there were two or more *campesino* leagues in many states and that there were eight or ten national *campesino* organizations with headquarters in Mexico City. While insisting that his administration had the responsibility "for ensuring that the problems of the agrarian classes shall be wholly resolved," the president declared that "there can be no resolution if bases of support are not established which can provide cooperation in reaching effective solutions." For this reason, he asserted that there must be "total unification" of the peasants and strict discipline in their agricultural operations, particularly with regard to their use of *ejido* credit.[34]

Cárdenas went on to enumerate problems of the *ejidos* within the Federal District and in other parts of the country:

> We know that here in the Federal District the parcels of land in many *ejidos* are extremely small and that they cannot resolve the economic problems of a family. We know that there are provisional donations of a hectare and a half, and donations of half a hectare for a peasant—donations completely insufficient and for which the Government must seek an immediate solution. We have other problems that we have come to be aware of as a result of

your help and as a result of observations that we have been able to make during our travels throughout the Republic.

Then he added: "But, as I said in the beginning, we cannot completely fulfill your program if in the first place we cannot depend on the unification of the peasant classes."[35]

Explaining that his government had not sought to use or to control the unification movement for Mexico's industrial laborers, Cárdenas insisted that a similar policy would be followed with regard to *campesino* affairs. He pledged to the delegates representing the agrarian communities of the Federal District that government intervention in their convention and in other *campesino* conventions would be restricted to measures designed to facilitate unification and to aid in transporting delegates and paying their expenses.

Denying that the federal government or the PNR would try to influence the election of *campesino* organization officials, the president declared: "The Government and the Party desire that the peasant organizations of the country shall have true autonomy so that in this form they can cherish an absolute confidence in the Government itself. It is necessary that there should be class consciousness among the peasants, and this class consciousness can be demonstrated only in the unification of all the peasants into a single unit. The Government only desires to facilitate this organization in order to carry to a conclusion the program that it has outlined for the benefit of the peasants of the country."[36]

Following the president's address, Portes Gil described the work of the PNR's Organizing Committee of Peasant Unification that had arranged the convention and had drawn up a plan consisting of a Declaration of Principles and a Program of Action. Regarding the content of these two documents, he explained that the basic ideas had been taken from Cárdenas's campaign speeches and from addresses the president had made after taking office. Portes Gil assured the delegates that "these fundamental points and orientations have been fully ratified by him, and many of them wholly dictated by him."[37] Although dwelling in length on such matters as eventual socialization of land, promotion of socialist education, state direction of the economy, and liquidation of alcoholism, the PNR head placed greatest emphasis on the importance of peasant unification. He declared:

> It is necessary, *campesinos*, that all of you understand that the unification of the proletarian class of Mexico is absolutely indispensable in order to go forward achieving the future social conditions to which you have full right; that this division, which unfortunately has been created in some states, is an important factor determining why the peasant class has not attained the place that it must attain and where it has the right to be; that this division should be ended; and that with all united under a single program, according to our laws and with full confidence in the Government of the Republic, we shall go forward little by little, winning these rights and acquiring the economic, cultural, artistic, and social benefits to which the peasants and the workers of the Republic are entitled.[38]

Portes Gil concluded his speech by urging the delegates to settle their petty quarrels and to return to their *ejidos* to continue the work of peacemaking and unification.[39]

Then Gabino Vásquez, chief of the Agrarian Department, spoke to the delegates, warning them against the false leaders who would seek to promote conflicts between workers and peasants and reminding them that peasants constituted the strongest group in the country.[40] After Sen. Ernesto Soto Reyes read the statutes drafted by the organizing committee, the delegates promptly approved the document with only a few minor changes.[41]

The convention closed on the following day, after electing a slate of officers to preside over the new peasant organization for the Federal District. The delegates also heard impassioned denunciations of *callista* failures and corruption under previous administrations.[42]

Within the next four months, following the pattern of the Federal District convention in Mexico City, similar conventions were inaugurated in Morelos, Aguascalientes, Zacatecas, San Luis Potosí, Tamaulipas, Nuevo León, Chihuahua, and Durango.[43] Although Cárdenas did not attend any of these meetings, Portes Gil, Graciano Sánchez, and Gabino Vásquez were usually present to denounce the consequences of peasant divisions and to describe the benefits that would accompany unification.

In all cases, the result was the same. Former peasant leagues were abolished or reorganized, and a state organization was created under loyal *cardenista* leadership. The guiding hand of party and government functionaries was quite obvious. For example, meetings of peasant leaders, state and municipal functionaries of the PNR, and representatives of the local government, to prepare for the Coahuila convention in February 1936, were held in Agrarian Department offices in Saltillo. There, under the direction of León García, representative of the Organizing Committee of Peasant Unification, plans were made for supervising the election of peasant delegates in each of the thirteen zones.

León García and his colleagues named a four-man committee consisting of representatives of the Agrarian Department, the League of Agrarian Communities, the PNR, and the state government for each zone. Not only were these committees responsible for supervising the conduct of elections for the naming of unification congress delegates, but they were also to assist the communities in presenting resolutions at the congress.[44] In no way were labor union officials involved in this government-sponsored campaign to unify Mexico's peasant organizations—an issue hotly resented by the ambitious, power-hungry Lombardo Toledano.

When Lombardo Toledano and his associates organized the CGOCM, they envisioned the eventual gathering of all peasant groups, as well as all labor unions, within one proletarian organization. The CGOCM actively sought to enlist peasant elements. The National Committee of Proletarian Defense, created in June 1935, included agrarian communities among the organizations entitled to send delegates to the National Congress of Labor Unification that created still another new organization, the Confederación de Trabajadores Mexicanos (CTM), in February 1936.

In view of Cárdenas's Cuautla resolution and the subsequent activities of the PNR's Organizing Committee of Peasant Unification, it was apparent that labor leaders, particularly Lombardo Toledano, were attempting to extend their organizing activities beyond acceptable limits. Consequently, CCM Secretary-General Graciano Sánchez decided that the time had come to halt organized labor's efforts to incorporate peasant groups within one proletarian organization.

On February 4, 1936, Sánchez (who was also a member of the Organizing Committee of Peasant Unification) dispatched a circular to all peasant leagues affiliated with the CCM.[45] The communication called attention to the fact that the National Committee of Proletarian Defense had convoked a congress of unification for the period of February 21 to 24. It pointed out that the Organizing Committee of Peasant Unification of the PNR was attempting to unite all peasants into the CNC as the best means of fulfilling Cárdenas's land reform projects.[46] In view of this peasant unification movement, the circular declared: "We make a formal call to you that precise instructions be sent to all agrarian communities and unions informing them that they should refrain from naming delegates to attend this congress."[47]

On February 23, a committee headed by Lombardo Toledano presented a report to the National Congress of Labor Unification condemning the action of Graciano Sánchez. Without criticizing Cárdenas, the report charged that certain political elements enjoying the confidence of the president had used their official influence to organize the peasants for their own personal or political interests. The Lombardo Toledano committee suggested that these efforts at peasant unification could only have one or two possible ends: to create a national peasant organization first and then to consolidate it with non-CTM labor groups in order to impose government control over the proletariat according to the principles of fascism, or to organize the peasants into a political force that would be incorporated into the PNR or the government with the objective of playing them off against organized labor.

Consequently, Lombardo Toledano's committee proposed a five-point resolution calling for the congress to take action to prevent these possible developments. The resolution declared that all elements of the Mexican proletariat should be unified within a single organization completely independent of the government. It also called upon all peasant groups to accept government assistance in economic, cultural, and technical matters, but to reject all attempts that might be made to use them for political purposes. Further, the committee stipulated that the congress should lodge a protest with the president against the activities of Graciano Sánchez and other elements of the PNR seeking to cause divisions within the laboring class and that it should request that Cárdenas order his subordinates to restrict their activities to providing economic, cultural, and technical assistance for the peasants while abstaining from using them for political purposes.

Finally, the resolution proposed that the congress "recommend to all groups represented in this congress and composed of *peones* living within *haciendas*, *ejido* members, and workers in agricultural industries, and all groups in general, that they should work actively among all the peasants of the Republic with the object of explaining to them the content and scope of the considerations on which these resolutions are based, to the end of avoiding exploitation of a political character of which they may be victims with grave prejudice to the unification of the national proletariat."[48]

Not only did the congress unanimously approve the report and the resolution of Lombardo Toledano's committee, but, on the following day, a committee on agrarian problems made detailed recommendations concerning the handling of peasant affairs. The most important recommendation proposed "that there be convoked in the shortest possible time a National Peasant Congress to which will be invited all the peasants of the country, including those groups sponsored by the PNR, in order to obtain their total unification; and, finally, to attempt by all possible means to separate the peasants from government control."[49]

The congress approved all recommendations of the committee on agrarian problems. On that same day, the congress adopted a body of statutes that outlined a long list of benefits to be sought for Mexico's peasant class,[50] declared that agrarian communities and peasant syndicates were eligible for CTM affiliation, called for the election of a secretary of peasant action to serve on the national committee, and specified that peasant groups should unite in each locality and eventually form a national peasant union that would be a part of the CTM.[51]

In response to CTM criticism of the CCM's peasant unification activity, Secretary-General Graciano Sánchez and other members of the CCM's central executive committee drafted and signed a stinging manifesto on February 25.[52] Refuting the charge that the CCM opposed proletarian unification the document explained that while the circular on February 4 had directed affiliated agrarian communities and peasant unions to abstain from participating in the congress convoked by the National Committee of Proletarian Defense such restrictions had not been imposed on its nonpeasant labor unions. The fact that these labor groups had been allowed to affiliate with the CCM was also cited as evidence that the CCM had not sought to isolate the peasants from other sectors of the proletariat.

The objective of the February 4 circular, the statement explained, "was none other than that there should be no obstruction to the unification being carried out by the Organizing Committee of Peasant Unification by means of state congresses, which certainly would have happened if the agrarian communities had been left free to attend the Proletarian Unity Congress."[53]

Dismissed as unfounded were charges that Mexico's peasants were being organized as a means of creating a type of corporative, fascist system that would impose government control over the proletariat. CCM leaders also rejected the accusation that the peasants would be converted into tools of the PNR and the government so that they might be played off against organized labor. At the same time, the statement noted that early in 1935, the CCM had cooperated with labor groups in an unsuccessful attempt to form a single national proletarian front. This document also pointed out that during the Calles crisis of June 1935, the CCM had not been invited to participate in the creation of the National Committee of Proletarian Defense. It had sent two delegates, however; and they had been turned away.[54]

When questioned by newspapermen concerning CTM attacks on the work of the PNR's Organizing Committee of Peasant Unification, Portes Gil issued a detailed statement.[55] He declared that the PNR supported wholeheartedly the creation of a single labor organization, such as Cárdenas had been recommending for some time. He expressed surprise, however, that the labor congress should have attacked the PNR for its successful campaign to unify Mexico's peasants.

Portes Gil insisted that the work of the organizing committee had followed strictly the directions outlined in Cárdenas's well-known Cuautla resolution and in the president's speech to the first unification congress composed of delegates from agrarian communities within the Federal District. "It is not correct, then, to allege that the peasants are being organized for political ends," Portes Gil declared; "and it is much less correct to charge that there are plans to align them against their class brothers, the city workers, or that the formation of a corporative fascist regime is desired as has been so thoughtlessly affirmed by some delegates to the recently held labor congress."[56]

Portes Gil's statement brought an immediate response from Secretary-General Lombardo Toledano and other secretaries of the CTM National Committee. In a document dated February 26, 1936, they declared:

> We are pleased to know that the PNR applauds without reserve the formation of a single organization of the workers of the Republic. We are equally pleased to know that the PNR is not organizing the peasants with political ends. Consequently, we hope that the congress, which this National Committee must convoke in the near future in compliance with a resolution of the Congress of Proletarian Unification calling for the formation within the CTM of a single organization of all the peasants in the country, will be attended by those peasants who are presently being organized for non-political purposes by the PNR.[57]

On the following day, peasant delegates who had attended the Proletarian Unity Congress and who had decided to cast their lot with the CTM met and agreed to invite all peasant groups not represented at the Proletarian Unity Congress to adhere to the CTM, to request that the national executive committee of the CTM immediately issue a manifesto addressed to all Mexican peasants inviting them to attend a national peasant congress to be held not later than May 1936, and to name an organizing committee that would work with other CTM officials in making preparations for the holding of a proposed congress.[58]

At the end of February 1936, Cárdenas was faced with an anomalous situation. The CCM, which consisted principally of peasant leagues but which also included some labor unions, was cooperating with the PNR and the government's Agrarian Department in the task of unifying peasants in each state as a preliminary step toward creating the CNC. At the same time, the recently established CTM, which consisted mainly of labor unions but which also included some peasant leagues, was not content with its near monopoly control over industrial labor. The CTM was planning to hold a congress for the purpose of bringing all peasant groups within its *campesino* organization, the CNC.

Without doubt, Cárdenas desired separately organized labor and peasant confederations that would look to him for support and over which he could exercise such control as might be necessary to keep them functioning in harmony with the objectives of his administration. The CTM's bid for control over *campesinos* as well as urban workers posed a direct threat to this plan, however; and behind the CTM action could be seen the clever hand of Lombardo Toledano.

To Cárdenas, the necessary course of action was abundantly clear: Lombardo Toledano and the CTM must be put in their place. On February 27, aboard the presidential train traveling from San Luis Potosí to Mexico City, the president told newspaper reporters:

The CTM must abstain from convoking the congress of peasants. Because of the special conditions of these people, the Government rising from the Revolution has considered and continues to consider that it has the obligation to patronize their organization. The PNR, in sponsoring the peasant assemblies that are being held in the various states of the Republic, has done no more, as the party of the Government, than to respect a resolution that was dictated by the Chief Executive.

The transformation of our system of production that covers problems such as the redistribution of the land, the financing of its new possessors, and their organization into collective units capable of guaranteeing to the country the supply of those articles that are necessary for the feeding of the people and for the development of our forces of agricultural production—this transformation, I say, implies a direct responsibility for the Revolutionary regime.

Consequently, if the CTM or any other organization should endeavor to organize the peasants on its own account and in competition with the Government's effort, far from succeeding it will accomplish nothing more than to hatch germs of dissolution, introducing among the peasants the internal strife that has brought such fatal results to the industrial proletariat.[59]

Despite Cárdenas's warning, the CTM continued to manifest a strong interest in peasant affairs. A report to the national council of the CTM, dated October 19, 1936, referred to previous difficulties with Portes Gil over the issue of calling a peasant congress. It recommended that the national council do something about the matter.[60]

Subsequent reports by the national committee of the

CTM made no further reference to such a meeting. Those reports, however, did indicate that CTM personnel were active in assisting both affiliated and nonaffiliated peasant groups in making applications for donations of land and water, securing protection from the "white guards" employed by the *hacendados*, and obtaining credit from the National Bank of Ejido Credit.[61] The reports also contained complaints of inefficiency and corruption on the part of Agrarian Department officials,[62] charging that some functionaries of this department had refused to take action on petitions submitted by CTM-affiliated groups merely because of their hostility toward the CTM.[63]

Although CTM leaders issued a circular on February 12, 1937, authorizing their peasant groups to send delegates to the unification congresses being convened by the PNR's National Committee of Peasant Unification,[64] they had little enthusiasm for such meetings. For example, in a report dated April 27, 1937, the national committee of the CTM mentioned the fact that CTM-affiliated peasants in Veracruz had been given permission to participate in that state's unification congress; but it also said: "Close observations of the facts demonstrate that this congress, as in the case of previous congresses held in other states of the Republic, suffered from most serious defects that should be corrected; otherwise the unification of the peasant class of our country will amount to no more than a bureaucratic function of a political character, while the peasant masses will receive no benefit from this class of assembly."[65] Thus the secretary-general of the CTM requested that the party leadership "establish the bases to which the congresses of peasant unification must adhere and . . . recommend them to the Organizing Committee of Peasant Unification, not only seeking to obtain the guarantees already indicated but so that the rural workers might feel the direct support of the laborers and manual workers composing the Confederación de Trabajadores Mexicanos, and might at the same time view the problem of peasant unification with an impersonal turn of mind and as an aspect of the unification of the proletariat of our country."[66]

There is no indication that this mission was attempted by the CTM leaders; but it is quite improbable that the organizing committee would have been receptive to such CTM meddling. Although CTM-affiliated peasant groups did continue to participate in state unification congresses, CTM leaders expressed the hope that creation of the proposed peasant confederation would open the way for cooperation between the two organizations. Therefore, during its First National Congress held from February 21 to February 25, 1938, CTM leadership reported that the CTM now possessed sizable numbers of organized agricultural workers and former hacienda peons who had received land by means of CTM efforts. Peasant unity, they insisted, must be achieved by membership in the CNC so that all the "producing masses" could benefit from and strengthen the Revolution.[67]

CCM Circular No. 37 revealed, however, that at least some CTM groups were following courses of action that could hardly be termed cooperative. Published without CCM authorization in the January 26, 1938, issue of *Excelsior*, this confidential document declared: "Contravening General Lázaro Cárdenas' high and noble aims in regard to the unification of the peasant class, as expressed in the presidential resolution of July 1935, the CTM has been carrying on an active and regrettable labor tending to disrupt the unity of the rural workers."[68]

For the information of affiliated organizations, the CCM document described in detail specific divisive acts by CTM groups in Aguascalientes, Durango, and Sinaloa. Leagues of agrarian communities and peasant unions in Aguascalientes and Durango had complained that their affiliates had not been invited to attend congresses convened by local CTM organizations. From Los Mochis, Sinaloa, came word that a group of nearly one thousand demonstrators organized by CTM elements had marched through the streets protesting recognition by the Central Board of Conciliation of peasant unions that had refused to adhere to the CTM.[69]

When questioned about relations with the CTM, a CCM spokesman, León García, replied that relations "could not be better." The incidents covered by the circular, he explained, had been provoked by CTM elements of a "secondary category."[70] About the same time, the CCM declared that the CCM circular should be ignored in the interests of unity. García added that the efforts toward worker unity being undertaken by President Cárdenas should not be contradicted.[71]

Evidence of conflict between peasants and politicians

over who would control the new national organization became apparent once more when Cárdenas held a conference with delegates to the constitutional assembly in the presidential palace shortly before they met in formal session. The president's advice to the delegates attending the conference, advice that he repeated in his address to the assembly on the following day, indicated that he wanted an organization directed at the national level by *cardenista* politicians. Since the peasant unification program had obvious political aims as well as socioeconomic objectives, one is not surprised by Cárdenas's determination to control this potentially powerful organization.

On March 1, 1936, only three days after stating that the CTM should not attempt to organize Mexico's peasants, Cárdenas arrived in Guadalajara to address the unification congress of Jalisco peasants.[72] Portes Gil and Graciano Sánchez had already opened the state congress on the previous day. Their speeches emphasized the importance of unifying Jalisco's two competing peasant leagues and held out promises of the benefits that would result from such action;[73] but Cárdenas's address contained more than a mere repetition of those remarks that congresses of this nature had come to expect from government, PNR, and CCM functionaries.[74]

Pointing out that the federal budget for 1936 provided increased funds for the Agrarian Department and that a total of 20 million pesos was being placed at the disposal of the National Bank of Ejido Credit, the president admitted that even these measures were insufficient for the purpose of adequately meeting the needs of Mexico's rural workers. He then announced that a special effort would be made to speed up the donation of land to peasants, especially to the peasants of Jalisco.[75] Such preferential treatment for the rural workers of this state was justified, according to Cárdenas, because for a long time they had been the victims of violence incited by large landowners. Therefore, he promised that, during the month of March, the Agrarian Department would send fifty engineers to Jalisco in order to intensify land distribution.[76]

The president also outlined a plan for providing greater protection for the peasants against armed attacks by their enemies, whom he identified as fanatic *cristero* bands, criminal plunderers, and the white guards employed by hacienda owners who opposed the government's land reform program.

Asserting that it was the duty of the government to protect the lives of the peasants, he promised that arms would be made available to them as soon as the congress had completed its task of creating a single *campesino* league for Jalisco.

Cárdenas specified, however, that peasants receiving arms would be organized into a type of military reserve that would be supervised by the regular army. Under this system, the president explained, rural workers would be able to defend themselves and their land while at the same time serving as auxiliaries of the army and as defenders of the nation's institutions. He emphasized that the armed peasants would have the particular responsibility of defending socialist schools. He declared that they should not only send their children to these schools but also "fraternize more with the teachers," whom he described as "the most faithful friends of the labor and peasant class." [77]

In the thirty months that followed the holding of the Guadalajara congress, the Organizing Committee of Peasant Unification continued holding meetings.[78] Finally, after a congress had been held in each entity of the federal republic and most of Mexico's *ejidatarios* and unionized farm laborers had been organized into territorial peasant leagues, the organizing committee issued a formal call on August 8, 1938, for delegates to the long-awaited constitutional assembly that would create the Confederación Nacional Campesina. August 28 was the date set for the opening of this assembly in the Emiliano Zapata Auditorium of the Casa Emiliano Zapata Auditorium of the Casa del Agrarista in Mexico City.[79]

On August 27, the ninety-six delegates representing thirty-two leagues of agrarian communities and peasant unions were received at the presidential palace. After greeting each one individually, Cárdenas proceeded to tell the delegates what was expected of them. Emphasizing that they should be vigilant to preserve class unity and to support the CNC officers who would be elected, the president insisted: "We need your unconditional responsibility and discipline so that we shall not see the spectacles that we have witnessed in some of the state leagues in which the officers have been divided by merely personal affairs."

Regarding the election of organization officials, Cárdenas insisted that he would make no recommendations. "You are absolutely free," he told the delegates, "to name as directors of the CNC those elements most identified with the agrarian movement and most capable of demanding your respect." Then, with a concluding admonition that the peasants "must not dedicate themselves to sterile struggles that only serve to delay the benefits of the Revolution," Cárdenas indicated that he was prepared to answer any questions that the delegates might wish to ask.[80]

As a result of this open invitation, the president heard some frank words that were probably unexpected. One delegate complained that the peasants "have noted the intervention of outsiders who seek to take advantage of their ignorance for political and personal ends." A peasant from Jalisco expressed his desire that offices in the CNC be given to "laboring peasants and not to meddling politicians"; and, referring to public officials who were allegedly desirous of obtaining posts in the new organization, he declared: "Mr. President, we desire that we be directed by peasants and that the public officials be prohibited from intervening in our confederation matters." Another delegate expressed the conviction that government party functionaries were seeking to usurp the rights of the peasants. Deputy Nabor Ojeda was reported to have charged that certain CCM leaders would be imposed upon the constitutional assembly and be given control over the peasants.[81]

In reply to these statements, Cárdenas asserted that the PRM, the recently reorganized party of the government, was composed of militants who sought to serve the workers. "In the assembly that you will have tomorrow," he explained, "you must direct your work carefully and do it with the greatest unity, without attacks against your own organization which is the PRM." Commenting on what he described as an apparent lack of "fraternity and serenity" among the delegates, he warned that divisions developing within the constitutional assembly would extend downward to the level of the agrarian communities. Regarding the question of whether officials of the CNC should be peasants or politicians, he advised: "You must think about whether it is more desirable that your directors should be peasants or friends of the peasants who until now have accompanied them in their struggles."

In view of these remarks, there could be little doubt that

Cárdenas intended that the CNC should be headed by trusted politicians. The fact that the president terminated the reception by inviting CCM leaders into his office for a conference suggested that last-minute preparations were to be made for the management of the assembly.[82]

At noon on August 28, 1938, Cárdenas arrived at the Casa del Agrarista accompanied by Luis I. Rodríguez, president of the PRM and chairman of the National Committee of Peasant Unification; Gabino Vásquez, chief of the Agrarian Department; Raul Castellanos, personal secretary to the president; and a group of presidential aides.

A committee headed by Graciano Sánchez greeted Cárdenas and escorted him into the Emiliano Zapata Auditorium where delegates, with the assistance of a *mariachi* band, hailed his entrance by singing the "Corrido del Agrarista."[83] The presence of leading PRM and CCM functionaries, together with members of the federal Congress, state governors, and other public officials, indicated the political significance of the occasion.[84]

After formally declaring the constitutional assembly to be in session, Cárdenas delivered an address in which he offered some advice as "your loyal and reliable friend."[85] Among other things, he recommended that the CNC elect officers of demonstrated ability who have "affection for the masses" and who could provide for representation of women on the central executive committee, develop a spirit of fraternity among all peasants of the country, bring into the organization those dissident peasant groups that had not joined state leagues, and prevent attacks by local peasant organizations against public authorities.

Emphasizing the importance of suppressing personal interests and cooperating with the government, the president declared:

> No one has the right to use the peasant organizations in order to satisfy personal interests. The peasant organizations, as well as those of labor, have a higher mission to fulfill: to watch over the realization of the social program that must uplift them spiritually and morally.
>
> It is necessary to understand that we are living under a revolutionary regime and that it is indispensable that the authorities and the sectors of society interested in the achievement of the aims of the Mexican Revolution should concur in pursuing the same

social end. Rather than advising sterile struggles, it is necessary to act within a healthy and responsible plan.[86]

In particular, Cárdenas advised the assembly to discuss the matter of whether directing officials of the CNC and state organizations should be allowed to campaign for public office during their period of incumbency or in the succeeding term. Regarding this subject, he observed that "experience has taught us that this is one of the main causes of the creation of divisions within the governing bodies themselves because there is always more than one candidate for the same popularly elected office; and, furthermore, they are distracted from their social work and from the interests of their organizations when they dedicate themselves to political activities."

He also called on the assembly to formulate minimum programs of action regarding education, vice, protection of infants, hygiene, women, agricultural techniques, combating diseases and plagues, organization of credit facilities, and "all that which may be of interest to you and which can strengthen the Nation."

Finally, concerning the structure and direction of peasant organizations, he urged that efforts be made to ensure majority rule and to maintain discipline in carrying out decisions. He predicted that in this manner "the peasant organization shall have contributed to the realization of the greatest ideal of the Mexican Revolution, which is to attain the implanting of the democracy of the workers within the country."[87]

Following the address by Cárdenas, Graciano Sánchez read a report covering the progress of agrarian reform in Mexico, the activities of the CCM since its founding, and the origin and achievements of the peasant unification movement.[88] Sánchez was followed by Luis I. Rodríguez, who praised the work of the Organizing Committee of Peasant Unification, emphasized the importance of the *ejido* in Mexico's planned economy, and explained the necessity of maintaining close relations between peasants, the army, industrial workers, the government, and the PRM.[89] After the remarks by Rodríguez, the delegates unanimously elected an unopposed slate of candidates for office.[90]

That evening, the second session of the day, delegates heard reports by two committees. One made recommendations concerning the CNC's proposed "Declaration of Principles" and its "Program of Action." The other dealt with the draft of the CNC statutes.[91] The Organizing Committee of Peasant Unification had prepared both of these documents.[92]

According to the proposed "Declaration of Principles," the CNC was created with the support of General Cárdenas for the purpose of "seeking the defense of the interests of the peasants and the spiritual and economic emancipation of all the organized rural workers." Other salient parts of the document included promises that the organization would struggle for a system of education oriented according to the doctrines of "scientific socialism," for recognition of the *ejido* as the basis of the country's agricultural policy, and for the eventual socialization of land "so that there will not remain a single Mexican peasant in need of land for the purpose of achieving his economic liberation."[93]

Divided into five articles, the recommended "Program of Action" called for modification of agrarian laws to provide greater benefits for the peasants in such matters as irrigation, reforestation, electrification, and donation of land. It also called for development of a school system that would provide education for the peasant class from the rural primary school level to higher education at a proposed proletarian university and for enforcement of minimum wage laws protecting peons, and establishment of credit and insurance institutions to meet the special needs of the peasant class.[94]

Among the principal provisions of the proposed statutes was the stipulation that the basic CNC units would be the *ejido*, the peasant union, and the cooperative—all of which would be grouped under the control of regional committees that would be subject to direction by the leagues of agrarian communities composing the national confederation. A general assembly composed of three delegates from each league would meet every two years or when called into special session by the CNC's central committee. Elected for two terms by the general assembly, the central committee would be composed of a secretary-general, secretary of treasury, secretary of agrarian action and peasant union organization, secretary of economic organization and agricultural credit, and secretary of education.[95]

One modification in the proposed statutes provided for four additional central committee posts: secretary of press and propaganda, secretary of feminine action, secretary of youth action, and chief clerk. Another change, which provoked a heated debate, concerned Article 12.

As originally drafted, Article 12 provided that a person holding the office of secretary within the governing body of a league of agrarian communities must "be a member of the organization and personally cultivate the land."[96] No such qualifications were proposed for secretaries serving at the national level; that is, those members of the central committee of the CNC. The committee responsible for reporting on the statutes therefore recommended that Article 12 should also establish qualifications for these national officials. The proposed change, however, was loosely phrased to provide that not only peasants who tilled the soil but also persons considered to be "perfectly identified with the peasant class" would be eligible.[97]

Despite the strong resistance of delegates who insisted that a peasant organization should be directed by bona fide peasants only and who feared that this provision would simply pave the way for imposition of nonpeasants in positions of national leadership, the assembly, by a majority of twenty-four, voted in favor of the committee's proposed change.[98] Consequently, political figures like Graciano Sánchez were not barred from national office in the organization.

Although the CCM secretary-general had declared that, with the organization of the CNC, he and other CCM leaders would "return to the ranks from which we came as loyal soldiers and servants of Mexico's agrarian cause" and would "turn over the burden of our responsibilities to hands better prepared than ours,"[99] the constitutional assembly ended its work early on the morning of August 29 with the election of Sánchez as secretary-general of the CNC and the election of León García, former CCM secretary of agrarian action, as his alternate.[100]

With the election of these officials, organization of the Confederación Nacional Campesina was completed more than three years after Cárdenas issued his call for peasant unification in the Cuautla resolution of July 9, 1935. During this period the great mass of Mexico's *ejidatarios* and members of peasant unions were organized into leagues affiliated with the CNC, although some still adhered to the CTM and others—particularly in the state of Veracruz—retained their affiliation with the weakened Liga Nacional Campesino "Ursulo Galván."[101]

Although Cárdenas did not achieve complete unification of all Mexican peasant groups, creation of the CNC represented a major accomplishment.[102] At the same time that he was promoting this unification activity, his administration was distributing more land to more *campesinos* than had been distributed under all previous presidents beginning with Carranza. Under Cárdenas, more than 17 million hectares were distributed to more than half a million *campesinos*; and the government loaned or expended millions of pesos for the benefit of its agrarian programs.[103]

Not only did most of Mexico's rural population provide political support for President Cárdenas, but organized *campesinos* could also be mobilized for military purposes if necessary. In view of the possibility that political issues might have to be settled with the use of force and as long as participation by machete-wielding, Mauser-armed peasants might determine the outcome of any military contest, the significance of Cárdenas's success in unifying Mexico's *campesino* organizations can easily be perceived. Not only were the organized *campesinos* a powerful deterrent to insurrection by counterrevolutionary elements, but also the CNC served as a counterbalance to other revolutionary groups within the PRM—especially the military and Lombardo Toledano's CTM. As suppliers of ballots and, if needed, of bullets, the CNC's *campesinos* helped guarantee that Cárdenas would remain in power for the full six years of his term and that he would be able to control the selection of his successor.

Four decades later, the CNC still plays an important role in the political and economic life of Mexico. President Lázaro Cárdenas is still remembered with genuine affection by the country's *campesinos* for the agrarian policies of his administration.

NOTES

1. Cárdenas has been the subject of two biographies by American

writers, but neither the Marxist-slanted *Reconquest of Mexico: The Days of Lázaro Cárdenas* by Nathaniel and Sylvia Weyl (London: Oxford University Press, 1939) nor the hero-worshipping *Lazaro Cardenas, Mexican Democrat* by William Cameron Townsend (Ann Arbor, Mich.: G. Wahr, 1952) provides objective treatment. A study of special importance is Joe C. Ashby's *Organized Labor and the Mexican Revolution under Lázaro Cárdenas* (Chapel Hill: University of North Carolina Press, 1967). The most important works in Spanish are Arnaldo Córdova, *La política de masas del cardenismo* (Mexico City: Ediciones Era, 1974), and Tzvi Medín, *Ideología y praxis política de Lázaro Cárdenas* (Mexico City: Siglo Veintiuno, 1972). For a Russian interpretation of the Cárdenas era, see Anatol Shulgovski, *México en la encrucijada de su historia: La lucha liberadora y antiimperialista del pueblo mexicano en los años treinta y la alternativa de México ante el camino de su desarrollo.*

2. See Lyle C. Brown, "Mexican Church-State Relations, 1933–1940," *A Journal of Church and State* 6 (Spring 1964): 202–222.
3. See Lyle C. Brown, "Los comunistas y el regimén de Cárdenas," *Revista de la Universidad de México* 25 (May 1971): 25–34; and Karl M. Schmitt, *Communism in Mexico: A Study in Political Frustration* (Austin: University of Texas Press, 1965), pp. 16–20. Also, see two articles by Albert Michaels: "Fascism and Sinarquismo: Popular Nationalisms against the Mexican Revolution," *A Journal of Church and State* 8 (Spring 1966): 234–250, and "Las eleciones de 1940," *Historia Mexicana* 21 (July–September 1971): 80–134.
4. Important research on Mexican peasant leagues has been done by Heather Fowler Salamini. See her "Adalberto Tejeda and the Veracruz Peasant Movement," in *Contemporary Mexico*, ed. James W. Wilkie, Michael C. Meyer, and Edna Monzón de Wilkie (Berkeley and Los Angeles: University of California Press, 1976), pp. 274–292, and her *Agrarian Radicalism in Veracruz, 1920–1938* (Lincoln: University of Nebraska Press, 1978).
5. Marjorie Ruth Clark, *Organized Labor in Mexico* (Chapel Hill: University of North Carolina Press, 1934), pp. 160–163. For important studies of Mexico's agrarian problems during this period, see Eyler N. Simpson, *The Ejido, Mexico's Way Out* (Chapel Hill: University of North Carolina Press, 1937), and Nathan L. Whetten, *Rural Mexico* (Chicago: University of Chicago Press, 1948). For histories of Mexico's peasant league movement, see Gerrit Huizer, *La lucha campesina en México* (Mexico City: Centro de Investigaciones Agrarias, 1970), and Moisés González Navarro, *La Confederación Nacional Campesina: Un grupo de presión en la reforma agraria mexicana* (Mexico City: B. Costa-Amic, 1968).
6. Emilio Portes Gil, *Quince años de política mexicana*, 3rd ed. (Mexico City: Ediciones Botas, 1954), pp. 475–482; also see statements by Marte R. Gómez and Emilio Portes Gil in *Mexico visto en*

siglo xx: Entrevistas de historia, ed. James W. Wilkie and Edna Monzón de Wilkie (Mexico City: Instituto Mexicano de Investigaciones Económicas, 1969), pp. 121–122, 581–582. All translations from the Spanish in this essay are mine.

7. The text of this document is published in Portes Gil, *Quince años*, pp. 477–481.
8. *Excelsior*, April 28, 1933.
9. See Victoriano Anguiano Equihua, *Lázaro Cárdenas, su feudo y la política nacional* (Mexico City: Editorial Eréndira, 1951), pp. 94–96.
10. *Excelsior*, June 8, 1933.
11. *El Nacional*, June 9, 1933.
12. See "Ponencia presentada ante la Convención Nacional del Partido Nacional Revolucionario en la Ciudad de Querétaro, por el Profesor Graciano Sánchez. Secretario de Acción Agraria de la Confederación Campesina Mexicana" printed in *Memoria de la Segunda Convención Nacional Ordinaria del Partido Nacional Revolucionario efectuada en la Ciudad de Querétaro del 3 al 6 de diciembre de 1933*, pp. 251–253.
13. Ibid., pp. 104–112.
14. Speech at Chihuahua, Chih., June 25, 1934, quoted in *La jira del General Lázaro Cárdenas: Sintesis ideológica*, p. 59.
15. Speech at Tres Palos, Gro., May 17, 1934, quoted in ibid., p. 63.
16. *Excelsior*, June 12, 1935.
17. Ibid.
18. This document is printed in *El Nacional*, June 14, 1935.
19. See Portes Gil, *Quince años*, pp. 521–522; *Excelsior*, June 17, 1935; and *El Nacional*, June 18 and 19, 1935.
20. See "Iniciativa sobre la unificación del proletariado mexicano," *Futuro* 2 (December 1934): 327–334.
21. Lombardo Toledano describes a midnight meeting with Cárdenas in a report recorded in "Sexta y última sesión, 29 de diciembre," in ibid., pp. 350–354.
22. See *El Nacional*, January 30 and 31, 1935.
23. Dated June 12, the text of the declaration was published in *El Día* on June 13. It is reported that copies of this declaration were delivered to *El Universal*, *Excelsior*, and *El Nacional* for publication of June 13 as paid announcements but all three refused to print the document. Although it was accepted for printing as a full-page announcement in *El Universal Gráfico*, at the last moment this Mexico City newspaper also decided not to publish it and money paid for printing costs was refunded. Not until Cárdenas had made plain the fact that Calles was not directing the government did these newspapers publish the declaration. Then they were forced to print it as part of another document, dated June 14, in which the public was informed of their earlier refusal to publicize the anti-Calles statement. See Marcelo N. Rodea, *Historia del movimiento obrero ferrocarrilero en México, 1890–1943* (Mexico City, 1943), pp. 564–565.

24. See Rodea, *Historia del movimiento*, pp. 571–574.
25. See Zeferino Narváez López, *Los campesinos de México en sus dos épocas* (Mexico City, 1949), pp. 122–123.
26. "Unificación campesina, acuerdo del señor general Lázaro Cárdenas, Presidente Constitucional de los Estados Unidos Mexicanos, expedido el 10 de julio de 1935," in *Cinco siglos de la legislación agraria (1493–1940)*, comp. Manuel Fabila (Mexico City: Los talleres de Industrial gráfica, 1941), p. 626.
27. Ibid.
28. Ibid.
29. Ibid., pp. 626–627.
30. *El Día*, July 31, 1935.
31. *El Universal*, August 4, 1935. For a description of the unification struggle in Veracruz, see Salamini, *Agrarian Radicalism in Veracruz*, pp. 132–134.
32. *El Nacional*, September 8, 1935.
33. The text of this address is printed in ibid.
34. Ibid.
35. Ibid.
36. Ibid.
37. The text of Portes Gil's address is printed in ibid.
38. Ibid.
39. Ibid.
40. Ibid.
41. Ibid.
42. *El Día*, September 9, 1935.
43. Statistics concerning peasant unification congresses are found in PNR, *Un año de gestión del Comité Ejecutivo Nacional, 1935–1936. Primer informe que rinde el Comité Ejecutivo Nacional del Partido Nacional Revolucionario a todos los sectores sociales del país*, pp. 57–61.
44. See *El Nacional*, January 28, 1936.
45. The text of this circular is printed in *Excelsior*, February 24, 1936.
46. Ibid.
47. Ibid.
48. The text of this document is printed in ibid.
49. The text of the committee's recommendations is printed in *Excelsior*, February 25, 1936.
50. Included among the proposed benefits were abolition of taxes and fees weighing heavily on peasants; guarantees against expulsion from the land they had cultivated; return of lands and waters that had been taken from them; abolition of rent payments; interest-free loans; freedom to hunt, fish, and cut wood if such practices were not inconsistent with conservation practices; free and sanitary lodging for agricultural workers at the cost of employers; expropriation of land without indemnification; distribution of land to peasants with preference given to those who have tilled it; modification of agrarian laws; elevation of the economic and social status of peasants; granting of the same rights

for peasants employed on *haciendas* as for other wage earners; and collective exploitation of the land by the peasants.

51. For the text of the CTM statutes, see CTM, *C.T.M., 1936–1941*, pp. 69–71.
52. This document is printed in *Excelsior*, February 26, 1936.
53. Ibid.
54. Ibid.
55. Portes Gil's statement is printed in *El Nacional*, February 26, 1936.
56. Ibid.
57. This statement is printed in *La Prensa*, February 27, 1936.
58. The resolution is printed in *Excelsior*, February 28, 1936.
59. Quoted in *El Universal*, February 28, 1936.
60. *C.T.M., 1936–1941*, p. 216.
61. Ibid., pp. 299, 334–335, 381–382, and 425.
62. Ibid., pp. 334, 382–384, and 426.
63. Ibid., pp. 631–632, 660–662, and 805–811.
64. *Excelsior*, February 13, 1937.
65. *C.T.M., 1936–1941*, p. 360.
66. Ibid. After studying this request, a reference committee, see ibid., p. 375, added the recommendation

> that the National Committee of Peasant Unification be told that the form in which the state congresses have been carried out does not satisfy the aim of unity of the Mexican proletariat: first, because the congresses are held under the influence of local political interests which are precisely those that have divided the peasants; and, in the second place, because we consider it to be indispensable that in these congresses there should be seated a representative labor delegation that . . . knows the peasant problems and at the same time can explain the general problems of the workers, thus attempting an approach that will facilitate national proletarian unity.

67. Ibid., p. 481. Lombardo Toledano's comments are in Wilkie and Wilkie, eds., *México vista en el siglo xx*, pp. 316–320.
68. *Excelsior*, January 26, 1938.
69. Ibid.
70. *Excelsior*, January 28, 1938.
71. Ibid.
72. The following message to Cárdenas was approved by the Jalisco congress during its opening session on February 29: "The Congress of Unification that has been inaugurated with representatives of all of the agrarian communities and peasant syndicates of the State of Jalisco, and which has the irrevocable purpose of liquidating all internal divisions, of loyally dedicating itself to resolve its class problems and to struggle for the betterment of the rural workers, and of collaborating without reservation with you in your noble organizing crusade, sends to you affectionate greetings, once more takes a firm stand with your government,

and hopes to have the honor of receiving you in this Congress." *El Día*, March 1, 1936.

73. Graciano Sánchez's speech is printed in *El Nacional*, March 1, 1936; parts of Portes Gil's speech are quoted in *El Día*, March 1, 1936.
74. The text of Cárdenas's address is printed in PRM, *Cárdenas habla*, pp. 33–34.
75. Ibid., p. 55. Also, see *Excelsior*, March 2, 1936, for an address made by Under Secretary of the Treasury Augustín Arroyo Ch. concerning the matter of financing agrarian reform.
76. Ibid., pp. 55–56. For detailed plans concerning the employment of these engineers, see Gabino Vásquez's speech printed in *El Nacional*, March 5, 1936.
77. PRM, *Cárdenas habla*, p. 57. Also, see Lic. José Muñoz Cota's address concerning socialist education and the peasant, *El Nacional*, March 6, 1936; and David L. Raby, *Educación y revolución social en México (1921–1940)*, trans. Roberto Gómez Ciriza (Mexico City: SepSetentas, 1974).
78. Portes Gil presided over a total of thirteen congresses before he was replaced as president of the PNR by Lic. Silvano Barba González, who supervised the organization of fifteen of these meetings. The last four congresses were held under the direction of Lic. Luis I. Rodríguez, who served as president of the official party after it had been transformed into the Partido Revolucionario Mexicano. See Graciano Sánchez's report to the constitutional assembly printed in *El Nacional*, August 29, 1938. As an example of a program for a typical state unification congress, see the program for the Sonora congress published in *El Nacional*, February 9, 1937.
79. The text of this convocation is printed in part in *Excelsior*, August 9, 1938. Also during the month of August there was a distinct trend toward greater harmony between the CTM and the CCM. Induced by the crisis that had been provoked by government expropriation of foreign-owned petroleum companies and by the reorganization of the official party, a joint statement of CTM-CCM solidarity was drawn up on August 9. See C.T.M.-C.C.M., *A todos los trabajadores de la república*. Also, on August 19 the national committee of the CTM issued a declaration describing an agreement between CTM and CCM deputies concerning plans for cooperation in the nomination of candidates for administrative posts and committee assignments within the Chamber of Deputies. See *El Nacional*, August 20, 1938.
80. This account of the meeting of Cárdenas and the constitutional assembly delegates is based on a report published in *Excelsior*, August 28, 1938.
81. See ibid.
82. See ibid.
83. One stanza of this folk song pays tribute to Cárdenas and his efforts to end strife among peasant groups:

México ya necesita sus tierras bien cultivadas,
Y Cárdenas, hombre recto, que está rigiendo nuestros destinos,
Vive en el corazón del pueblo mexicano.
Ay, ay, luchando por nuestro anhelo murieron muchos hermanos,
Ya no queremos más luchas entre hermanos.

84. See *El Nacional*, August 29, 1938.
85. The text of this address is published in ibid.
86. Ibid.
87. Ibid.
88. The text of his address is printed in *El Nacional*, August 29, 1938.
89. See ibid. for the text of Rodríguez's address.
90. Ibid
91. Ibid.
92. For the texts of these documents as originally proposed, see *Declaración de principios, programa de acción, y estatutos de la Confederación Nacional Campesina* (Mexico City, 1966).
93. See ibid., pp. 3–4.
94. See ibid., pp. 4–11.
95. See ibid., pp. 11–20. Among the powers conferred upon the central committee by Article 8 was that of appointing "the number of inspectors that may be necessary so that they may travel continuously throughout the Republic orienting the Regional Committees in their functions and, in general, keeping watch to see that all organs of the Confederation . . . make intense propaganda in order to keep alive the spirit of unification of the peasant class of the country and so that the comrades who are designated temporarily to occupy the directing offices of the organization do not turn away from the objectives of unification or become corrupt."
96. See ibid., p. 14.
97. *El Nacional*, August 29, 1938.
98. Ibid.
99. See *El Nacional*, August 29, 1936.
100. Ibid. For a complete list of CNC officers, see *Excelsior*, August 30, 1938.
101. The National Peasant League "Ursulo Galván" denounced what it termed "pretended peasant unification" and charged the CNC with defrauding "the aspirations of the authentic peasant movement and the sincere proposals of President Cárdenas for unification of the proletariat." At the same time, it declared that the National Peasant League "Ursulo Galvan" "had fought for, is seeking, and will achieve true unification of the laboring peasant masses independent of the influence and the tutelage of politics and in opposition to the political leaders who call themselves 'friends of the peasant.' " Quoted in *Excelsior*, August 30, 1938.
102. See Jesús Silva Herzog, *El agrarismo mexicano y la reforma agraria: Exposición y crítica* (Mexico City: Fonda de Cultura Económica, 1959), p. 406.

103. See Whetten, *Rural Mexico*, pp. 125–127; James W. Wilkie, *The Mexican Revolution: Federal Expenditure and Social Change since 1910* (Berkeley and Los Angeles: University of California Press, 1970), pp. 76, 138–139.